DAVID J. RANDALL

CHRISTIANITY

IS IT TRUE?

ANSWERING QUESTIONS
THROUGH REAL LIVES

CF4•K

10 9 8 7 6 5 4 3 2 1
Copyright © David J. Randall 2018

paperback ISBN 978-1-5271-0236-1
epub ISBN 978-1-5271-0288-0
mobi ISBN 978-1-5271-0289-7

Published in 2018
by
Christian Focus Publications, Ltd.
Geanies House, Fearn,
Ross-shire, IV20 1TW, Scotland.
www.christianfocus.com

Cover design by Pete Barnsley

Printed and bound by Bell and Bain,
Glasgow

FSC® C007785
MIX
Paper from responsible sources

CONTENTS

Introduction 7

1. A Copyright Dispute 13

2. Mr Valiant-for-truth 21

3. Making Progress 29

4. Persevere 37

5. 'Dr Livingstone, I presume' 47

6. To God be the Glory 55

7. 'She's Game, Boys' 63

8. The Secret Room 71

9. Behind the Wardrobe 79

10. Running the Race 89

11. 'Whoever Loses his Life ...' 99

12. 'PTL' (Praise the Lord) 107

Epilogue 115

Introduction

This book tells the stories of twelve individuals who (like the people listed in Hebrews 11) lived 'by faith'. The writer of Hebrews believed that the stories of people like Noah, Abraham and Moses can inspire us. These were people who achieved great things through faith.

After listing many such heroes of faith, he went on in Hebrews 12:1-2 (as paraphrased by Eugene Peterson): 'Do you see what this means – all these pioneers who blazed the way, all these veterans cheering us on? It means we'd better get on with it. Strip down, start running – and never quit! … Keep your eyes on Jesus' (MSG).

A few verses further on, it says, 'When you find yourselves flagging in your faith, go over that story again … that will shoot adrenaline into your souls!' (Hebrews 12:3 MSG)

What story? He was referring to the story of Jesus as we find it in the Bible. It's the story of the greatest life ever lived, the most significant death ever died and the most momentous victory ever won. It's all about God Himself coming from heaven to save us and help us.

It's also true that the stories of notable people from the centuries of Christian history can help us to follow in their footsteps – trusting Jesus as our Saviour and living our lives for Him.

The twelve people whose stories are told in this book were very different from each other:

- *they come from different backgrounds: some had a privileged start in life; others knew hardship and poverty*
- *they come from different periods of history, ranging from the sixth century to the twenty-first*
- *they vary in nationality: Scottish, English, American, Dutch, Irish*
- *they represent varied areas of life and work: medicine, politics, athletics, literature, exploration, campaigning, education*
- *some had a comfortable life; others experienced suffering, injustice and violent death*
- *they were different in personality: some were forthright; others more reserved*
- *and their labours achieved different things: the liberation of slaves, resistance to the Nazis, care for the sick and the spreading of the gospel*

The thing they had in common is that they did what they did 'by faith'. None of them would want us to praise or idolise them. They would share the desire of Paul when he encouraged his readers to follow him insofar as he followed Christ (1 Corinthians 11:1). They might say what was said by the writer of Psalm 115:1, 'Not to us, O LORD, not to us but to your name give glory'.

So this book seeks to encourage you to commit your life to Christ while you are young and to stand by that commitment in a world where it is not easy to do so. There are many pressures to turn away from the gospel of Christ and for many the teenage years are years when an earlier faith is questioned and, in some cases, abandoned.

It has been said that during these years of transition from childhood to adulthood, one's religious beliefs, like many childish ideas, are likely to be subjected to the test of three questions:

- *is it true?*
- *does it work?*
- *is it worth it?*

The first question, reflected in our title, is the big one: is Christianity true? Sometimes people will say that it must be true because it brings joy, peace and comfort, but a moment's thought would lead you to question that conclusion. After all, belief in the tooth fairy or the man in the moon might bring some people happiness – but that doesn't prove that they exist.

C. S. Lewis (the subject of chapter 9) pointed out that if Christianity is untrue, no honest person should have anything to do with it, even if such a belief might prove helpful, but if it is true, then it calls for our faith and commitment whether it brings comfort or not.[1]

Lewis himself came to believe that it is the truth, and the others described in this book also believed in the truth of Christianity. They also demonstrate that it works in real life, and they would all answer the third question (is it worth it?) with a resounding Yes.

Whether you have been brought up to believe or not, I hope that reading about these people, who are great role models for today, will help to convince you of the truth, relevance and value of commitment to Jesus Christ.

---

1. www.brainyquote.com/quotes/c_s_lewis_164517 (accessed 27.6.18).

Many of the most important issues of life are settled when you are young. Obviously you may change your mind on some things later on, but the choices you make when you are young often have a lasting impact on your whole life. It is usually when you are young that you choose a husband or wife. It's when you are young that you choose a job or career ambition. Possibly your political outlook and your recreational interests are chosen when you are young, and the same goes for the most important matter of all – your response to the call of Christ.

Clearly, people can become Christians at any age or stage of life and it is never too late to respond to Christ, but for many it is the choice made in early years that sets the pattern for the future.

Today there are many pressures that might lead people to abandon Christianity. You may hear of famous people dismissing it and some of your friends may say that it's not cool to believe in Jesus, go to church, resist temptation, and so on. We hope that these stories may help you to – what was it? – 'start running and never quit'. They are real life stories and as we look at them we will see answers to the questions: is it true, does it work, and is it worth it?

Probably none of us is going to be an Eric Liddell or a Corrie ten Boom, but God calls us to trust in Him and serve His kingdom.

- If we ask, 'Is Christianity true?' – Jesus said, 'I am the truth' (John 14:6).
- If we ask, 'Does it work?' – He said in the same breath, 'I am the way'; His way works (as we will see in the stories that follow).
- And if we ask, 'Is it worth it?' – He also said, 'I am the life' – and what could be more 'worth it' than to trust and follow Him?

We might have called this book *Servants of God*, using a phrase from a hymn written by someone who is not one of the twelve described here, Charles Wesley. He was, interestingly, the youngest of seventeen children – something I don't expect to be true of many readers. He wrote more than 6,000 hymns and many of them are still sung frequently – hymns such as 'Love divine', 'O for a thousand tongues to sing' and 'Hark! the herald angels sing'. Another starts with the words:

Ye servants of God, your Master proclaim,
And publish abroad his wonderful name.[2]

The twelve 'servants of God' whose stories are told in this book all wanted to tell out the 'wonderful name' of Jesus, and since He chose twelve disciples there's a good justification for choosing twelve for this book.

If you've read *Alice in Wonderland*,[3] you may remember the point where Alice asked, 'Which way do I go from here?' The answer of the Cheshire Cat was, 'That depends a great deal on where you want to get to'.

If you want to find fulfilment and make the most of your life, the way to go is the way of trusting and following Jesus. I hope this book will help you to do so.

---

2. Hymn, 'Ye servants of God', by Charles Wesley, 1707-88.

3. Lewis Carroll and Alison Jay, *Alice's Adventures in Wonderland* (West Sussex: Old Barn Books edition, 2017), 97.

A Copyright Dispute
Columba: Sailor and Evangelist

If you hear the word 'Scotland', what comes to mind? It might be bagpipes, kilts or haggis. Or it might be people like John Logie Baird (inventor of television), Alexander Graham Bell (inventor of the telephone) or Sir James Simpson (discoverer of chloroform).

For some people, however, there's another association with Scotland – the Loch Ness Monster!

Do you believe it exists? Or is it merely an invention of the tourist industry? If it is a myth, it is one with a long pedigree, because (believe it or not) back in the year 565 Columba of Iona said he saw it.

Columba's biographer, a man called Adamnan, wrote about Columba's travels in Scotland[1] and said that he came upon some Picts who were burying a man who had died after being bitten by a water monster while he was swimming. Columba sent one of his followers to fetch a boat from the other side of the loch and this man too was attacked by the monster. According to the story, the monster came at him with a huge roar and with open jaws, but Columba made the sign of the cross and the monster fled.

---

1. *Vita Columbae (Life of Columba)* probably written between 697 and 700.
https://en.wikipedia.org/wiki/Adomnan (accessed 27.6.18)

Whatever be the truth of that story, what *is* true is that Columba was one of the Irish monks who brought Christianity to Scotland. His name means 'dove' and he is often known in historical accounts as Saint Columba. This comes from the later practice of canonisation, in which the (now Roman Catholic) church recognises certain people as very special. In more common usage the word 'saint' signifies an unusually holy or virtuous person (for example, we talk about someone having the patience of a saint), but in the Bible it is the word for a Christian. It refers not to some 'higher class' of Christian but to anyone who follows Jesus as Saviour and Master. The word 'Christian' is only found three times in the Bible; the normal word for followers of Jesus is 'saints' (used sixty-two times in the AV New Testament). All Christians are saints, so let's just call Columba Columba.

He was born into a noble family in County Donegal in 521 and educated in monasteries in Ireland before he later established several more himself.

It is often said that God moves in a mysterious way His wonders to perform.[2] He may bring about His purposes through an envied coat of many colours (Joseph), a great fish that could swallow and then spew out a human being (Jonah) or even a simple veggie diet (Daniel). In Columba's case, it was a copyright dispute.

He loved books, and he loved to obtain books of Psalms, whole Bibles or other edifying books for his students. Another monk, Finnian, allowed Columba to see a Psalm book he owned, and Columba was so impressed by it that he copied it all out for himself.

When Finnian discovered this, he was angry and demanded that the copy be handed over to him. Columba refused and a copyright dispute ensued; this was more than a thousand years before there were official copyright laws. It was taken for decision

---

2. Hymn by William Cowper, 1731-1800.

to the king of Ireland who ruled that just as a calf belongs to the mother cow, a copy of a manuscript belongs to the owner of the original.

Columba, however, refused to hand over the copy and the matter (along with some other disputes) escalated into a military confrontation which resulted in the death of about three thousand people. Columba was held to be responsible for these deaths and, strange as it may seem, this incident turned out to be the thing that led to Columba's perilous journey across the sea and the planting of the gospel in Scotland.

He was censured by the church and he might have been excommunicated if it hadn't been for the intervention of another monk called Brendan.

But Columba's own conscience troubled him and he decided to go into exile, with the goal of winning as many converts as the number of people who had died in the horrible battle he had caused.

So it was that in the year 563 Columba, along with twelve companions, set sail in a little boat (a coracle) and eventually settled on the small island of Iona off the west coast of Scotland.

There he built a monastery which would be his home for the rest of his life and he established a Christian community in which he exercised his own gifts as a preacher and pastor. He studied, he prayed, he practised self-discipline, and Iona became the base for the evangelisation of the Scots and Picts, through which much of the religious and social life of Scotland eventually came to be Christianised.

Iona was a missionary base and churches were established in many places as he covered many miles and evangelised vast areas of the country. When Columba wasn't on such journeys, he received many visitors, some of whom came for spiritual or material help.

Adamnan described Columba's older years (he lived to the age of seventy-six) in which he slept on bare rock and had a diet of barley, oat cakes and water. When he couldn't travel any longer, he returned to the copying of manuscripts and we are told that on the day before he died he had copied out the words of Psalm 34:10 – 'Those who seek the Lord lack no good thing' – and then he stopped and said someone else would have to take over. When people gathered for prayers early on the next morning, they found Columba breathing his last.

It was on one of his missionary journeys that the Loch Ness 'Monster' incident took place. He was on his way to see Brude, King of the Picts, at his castle near Inverness. Brude was impressed by Columba and later professed Christianity, although it was probably an associate of Columba's who witnessed to the king. This was the Brendan we mentioned earlier, and as he proclaimed the message of the gospel, Brude asked the question, 'What shall I find if I accept your gospel and become Christ's man?'

It is a reasonable question to ask. It is always sensible to check out the consequences of decisions we are asked to make, including our response to the gospel. Jesus Himself encouraged people to count the cost. He said, 'If anyone would come after me, let him deny himself and take up his cross and follow me' (Mark 8:34) – and when Jesus spoke these words, taking up a cross was not a metaphor! The cost might be high and in fact most of the original disciples of Jesus did not die peacefully in their beds.

Brendan's answer to King Brude was that if he became a Christian he would 'stumble on wonder upon wonder, and every wonder true.'[3] These early missionaries emphasised the truth of the gospel. They bore not undertaking such risky travels and making such sacrifices in order to pass on 'nice myths' or 'feel-

---

3. 'What the Gospel means Today' by James S. Stewart in *Man's Dilemma and God's Answer* (S.C.M. Press, 1944), 159-176.

good stories' which might or might not be true but brought some comfort and solace.

In our introduction we spoke about three questions that are raised in the minds of many teenagers about Christianity, especially if they have been brought up to believe in Jesus. The first is the question, 'Is it true?'

That's crucial. I mean, belief in some imaginary friend or Santa Claus or fairies at the bottom of the garden might bring some degree of joy, comfort and contentment, but that doesn't mean they really exist. The apostle Peter wrote, 'We did not follow cleverly devised myths when we made known to you the power and coming of our Lord Jesus Christ' (2 Peter 1:16). He went on to emphasise that he and the other apostles were eye-witnesses of the things they were reporting.

Jesus was a real man who lived a real life, met real people, performed real miracles, died a real death, won a real victory over death and the devil, and has a real gospel for all times.

That's what Brendan was emphasising. If you become a Christian, you will discover wonder upon wonder, and every wonder true. A colleague of mine has said that there is only one good reason to believe in the Christian faith and that's if it's true. There may be some people who are comforted by myths and fables, but Christianity is neither a myth nor a fable. It is God's truth; in fact, Jesus Himself said, 'I am the truth' (John 14:6).

A humanist once suggested that Christians often forget to argue that Christianity is true. He said we sometimes concentrate on arguing that Christianity brings comfort and has good consequences and may even meet certain psychological needs to believe in something or someone.[4]

And of course Christianity does have enormous consequences. It is through the gospel of Christ that so many of the social and

---

4. Quoted by Joan Wragg, *Choice for Nowhere Men* (Scripture Union, 1969), 79.

intellectual advances of mankind have been made, whether you think of the way in which healthcare and education have been the normal results when the gospel has been established in any place, or of its social effects in the (eventual) abolition of slavery, the establishment of democracy and the development of science.

However, all of that depends on the truth of Christianity. What we are invited to embrace is not a set of nice ideas but a message based on the facts of the life, death and resurrection of Jesus Christ.

On one occasion the apostle Paul was dismissed as a deluded madman. That was the verdict of a Roman governor called Festus, but Paul responded by saying that he wasn't out of his mind; he said, 'I am speaking true and rational words' (Acts 26:25).

He went on to say in verse 26 about the foundational events of Christianity that they were not 'done in a corner'. There may be some belief systems that base themselves on secret events that lie beyond the scope of investigation; Christianity is not one of them.

And when Columba, Brendan and others brought the gospel to Scotland, they too were bringing a 'true and rational' message that invites our response to the living God who says to us as to the first disciples, 'Repent and believe' (Mark 1:15). And if we decide to trust and follow Him, we will discover wonder upon wonder.

One of Charles Spurgeon's stories concerns a poor minister who sometimes received an envelope containing £5 with the words printed on the outside, 'More To Follow'. It came from a philanthropist who gave a friend the (then vast) sum of £100 to be distributed a little at a time. So the minister would periodically receive the £5 note with that message, 'More To Follow'. Spurgeon used the story to illustrate the way in which God sends 'one blessing after another' (John 1:16; NIV).

It's the message given long ago to King Brude: if you become a Christian, you will come upon wonder upon wonder, and every wonder true. We can thank God that He moved in a mysterious way – even through a copyright dispute – to motivate Columba to bring the gospel over the sea to Scotland.

Columba was also a poet and one of his hymns has been sung by many people over the centuries since he brought Christianity to Scotland. We conclude this chapter with the words of that hymn which includes a reference to the kind of 'heroes' featured in this book but more importantly directs our attention to the Saviour whom he served and who invites us to trust and obey Him.

> Christ is the world's Redeemer, the lover of the pure,
> The fount of heavenly wisdom, our trust and hope secure,
> The armour of his soldiers, the Lord of earth and sky,
> Our health while we are living, our life when we shall die.
>
> Christ has our host surrounded with clouds of martyrs bright,
> Who wave their palms in triumph and fire us for the fight,
> For Christ the cross ascended to save a world undone
> And suffering for the sinful, our full redemption won.
>
> Down in the realm of darkness he lay a captive bound
> But at the hour appointed he rose, a victor crowned;
> And now, to heaven ascended, he sits upon the throne,
> In glorious dominion, his Father's and his own.
>
> Glory to God the Father, the unbegotten One;
> All honour be to Jesus, his sole-begotten Son
> And to the Holy Spirit— the perfect Trinity.
> Let all the worlds give answer: 'Amen—so let it be!'[5]

---

5. Hymn from Church Hymnary Revised Edition (Oxford University Press, 1927), 179.

TALKING POINTS

1. How does Columba's life illustrate the hymn that says, 'God moves in a mysterious way his wonders to perform'?

2. Could you explain the difference between believing in Jesus and believing in an imaginary friend or Santa Claus?

3. Do you agree with the statement, 'There's only one good reason to believe in Christianity and that's if it's true'? See 2 Peter 1:16 and Acts 26:25.

A PRAYER

Thank you, Lord, for Columba and others who left their own homes and endured many trials in order to spread the gospel. As the message is good news for sharing, we pray that you will help all who are spreading the gospel today. May many more people come to know that Christianity is true and rational.

Mr Valiant-for-Truth
John Knox: From Galley-Slave to National Reformer

The phrase 'anything for a quiet life' describes the attitude of some people who want to avoid all argument and controversy, people who will meekly agree with anything simply to avoid conflict. If you take a different view, especially on something political or religious, they'll just trot out their motto, 'Well, OK; anything for a quiet life'.

John Knox was not a member of that club! He lived in the sixteenth century and his life was full of activity, controversy and conflict. If people refer to him at all nowadays, it's usually in negative terms. He is caricatured as a joyless individual and sometimes when people refer to some feature of life in Scotland that is too strict for them, they'll dismiss it as 'shades of John Knox'.

Well, John could indeed be severe and even dour sometimes, but we do need to remember that he lived in tempestuous times. Life didn't have the luxuries that we enjoy now (not even an electric light to switch on) and people needed steel in their character if they were not to be walked over or blown away.

Much of his life was spent in religious controversy, and we need to remember that, unlike the society in which most of us live today, society in the sixteenth century was very much dominated by religious issues. The church was powerful in society and most of the big political events of the times had matters of religious belief behind them.

It was in such a time that John was born about 1514 in the town of Haddington (fifteen miles east of Edinburgh) and it was in such a time that his influence was to shape Scotland for generations to come.

As to the facts of his life: he studied in St Andrews and then became a priest. He also worked as a private tutor and for a time he preached in St Andrews, but in 1547 the town was besieged by eighteen French galleons in a war that had to do with royal marriages and political intrigues.

John was taken prisoner and for nineteen months was made to serve as a galley-slave (with 120 others) – chained to a bench and made to row throughout the day under threat of the lash.

This was the beginning of about twelve years of exile from Scotland. Later he spent some years in England (1549–1554), ministering in London, Newcastle and Berwick, but when Queen Mary came to the throne of England, she started a reign of terror in which nearly 300 people who wanted to reform the church were slaughtered (Mary came to be known as Bloody Mary because of this fierce persecution).

John then moved to Geneva where he met John Calvin, from whom he learned much about reformed theology and presbyterian church government. He felt guilty about his flight from Scotland and later wrote about it, 'I have in the beginning of this battle appeared to play the faint-hearted and feeble soldier, yet my prayer is that I may be restored to the battle again.'[1]

---

1. Iain H. Murray, *A Scottish Christian Heritage* (Edinburgh: Banner of Truth, 2006), 12.

Well, that prayer was certainly granted. He was called back to Scotland, arriving at Leith in May 1559, and he set about the task of rebuilding the church on scriptural foundations.

He and the other reformers in Scotland and in Europe saw that many abuses had crept in to the church over the years. They believed that neglect of the Bible had led to many practices that were wrong – things like buying favour for your departed relatives by giving money to the church or going on special pilgrimages. There was the practice of praying to the Virgin Mary, belief in purgatory and the idea that in 'the Mass' Christ's sacrifice is made over and over again, along with the strange notion that the bread and wine are miraculously changed into the actual body and blood of Christ.

The population of Scotland then was about 800,000 but there was a surprisingly high number of priests – about 3000 – and many of them, instead of setting a good example for other people, lived lives that were far from being Christ-like. Although priests were supposed to be celibate, some fathered illegitimate children.

Some of the priests were illiterate, few thought of preaching from the Bible and there was a crying need for the church to be reformed according to the truth of God's Word.

Shortly after his return to Scotland, Knox became the minister of St Giles' Cathedral in Edinburgh (1560-72), sometimes preaching to as many as 3,000 worshippers. Unfortunately it was before the day of sound recordings and we can only imagine the strength and conviction with which he proclaimed God's truth.

As with the reformers generally, he believed in salvation by God's grace through faith in Christ alone. It has been written of him: 'In contrast to the representation some give of him as a man who chiefly thundered out judgments, he describes himself rather as an assistant at a banquet of blessing where the Saviour himself is the host.'[2]

This is what John Knox and the other reformers believed, and they were prepared to do what it took to re-assert this faith, whatever the difficulties. The struggle was intense; the reformer, George Wishart, for whom John Knox had acted for a time as bodyguard, was burned at the stake in 1545.

Eventually, to cut a long story short, in 1560 the Scottish parliament established Protestantism as the religion of Scotland. Knox was himself responsible for drawing up the Scots Confession which was ratified by Parliament and he was really the father of the reformed church in Scotland.

According to the reformers, the church should be characterised by three things: the faithful preaching of the Bible, the proper administration of the sacraments (baptism and communion) and the exercise of discipline. A congregation was to be ruled by its elders and have the right to call its own minister.

In the political life of the nation, Mary Queen of Scots had become queen on the death of her father when she was only six days old, but she had lived many years in France. In 1561 she returned to Scotland, and she was determined to hold to the old (Roman Catholic) religion. This started the period of the famous conflict between John Knox and the Queen of Scots.

On the very first Sunday after her return from France, Mary requested that Mass be celebrated at Holyrood and the following Sunday Knox denounced this action publicly. Over the next six years, Knox and Mary had several stormy meetings.

Eventually, Mary's personal circumstances caused her huge trouble. Her first husband, Lord Darnley, died in suspicious circumstances and then she married the Earl of Bothwell who

2. Ibid, 21.

was probably involved in Darnley's death. This led to more controversy between the Protestant forces and Mary's Catholic supporters and she was forced to abdicate.

She was imprisoned in Loch Leven Castle but managed to escape. After a failed endeavour to regain the throne, she fled south to seek the help of her cousin, Queen Elizabeth of England. Elizabeth, however, kept Mary as a prisoner for twenty years and eventually had her executed in 1587.

Knox himself went back to St Andrews for about a year, preaching nearly every day although he was growing weak by that time, and he later returned to Edinburgh where he died peacefully in 1572. He was buried beside St Giles' Cathedral (under what is now a car park) and it was said of him, 'Here lies a man who in his life never feared the face of man.'[3]

Such was the tumultuous life of John Knox, a religious reformer, a preacher of God's message of salvation, a believer in education and a man who was not ashamed to own his Lord or defend His cause, whatever opposition there might be.

He was a man of prayer. He was a man of the Bible. He believed that God is sovereign over everything and he exulted in the message of grace which he loved to preach. In his last days, he would sometimes be confused about what day of the week it was and, thinking it was Sunday, he would make as if to go out to preach again. So was the proclamation of God's truth part of the fibre of his being.

One of his goals was that every part of Scotland should have a church and a school. He was 'way ahead of his times in the desire that people should be educated; he wrote to the nobles of the country, 'Of necessity it is that your honours be most careful for the virtuous education and godly upbringing of the youth of this

---

3. Steven J. Lawson, *John Knox* (Tain: Christian Focus, 2014), 107.

realm, if you seek the advancement of Christ's glory or desire the continuance of His benefits to the generation following.'[4]

One of our recurring questions in this book is the question of whether Christianity makes any difference to anything. John Knox's life shows that it certainly does. It is what we think and believe in our hearts that makes us what we are.

As we have said, modern society is very different from what it was in Knox's day. Religion for many is merely on the periphery of life; others want to dismantle our Christian heritage from the past. But, as Proverbs 9:10 says, it is the fear of the Lord that is the beginning of wisdom; if we reject belief in God, we cut off the branch on which we are sitting.

There was once a missionary who came upon a tribe of moon-worshippers. He was surprised; he had heard of sun-worshippers but never moon-worshippers. When he asked people why they worshipped the moon and not the sun, he was told that they honoured the moon because it shines at night when we're badly in need of light, while the silly old sun shines in the daytime when we have plenty of light anyway! It hadn't occurred to them that the moon only reflects light from the sun and that we live and move and exist only because of the light and heat of the sun.

Later in history, Mary Slessor, another of the subjects of this book, was concerned that many people were turning away from the gospel message that had brought them such benefits. In March 1909 she wrote in a letter, 'May God in His mercy save us from ever becoming a Christless nation! May the fate of other churches and nations who forget God never be ours.'[5]

That could be our prayer for our country today.

---

4. Quoted in Banner of Truth magazine, Issue 110 (November 1972), 10.

5. Bruce McLennan, *Mary Slessor – A Life on the Altar for God* (Tain: Christian Focus, 2014), 233.

Is it already too late? There are many signs in society of the results of godlessness. Unfortunately it seems as if unbelievers have huge influence in politics, the media and education, but it was a politician who once asked a colleague if he could say when Britain's decline in values began. His friend answered immediately, 'The day when people stopped going to church.'[6] Well obviously there wasn't any single day, and it's not just the ritual of church attendance that counts; he was referring to the faith and reverence for God that lies behind that. The same politician (one-time Prime Minister Lord Home) said that he didn't despair because Christianity is the truth and the future is ultimately in God's hands.

Do you know the old saying about the best time to plant an apple tree? When is that? Ten years ago! But the second best time is today. We can each put our trust in the Lord and His Word and seek to point others in the same direction.

Heroes like John Knox set us a great example.

---

8. Quoted from Lord Home's autobiography by the late Rev Tom Swanson in the church magazine of the West Parish of Inverness, March 1981.

TALKING POINTS

1. John Knox sought to 'stand firm' for God and His truth. Consider how he lived out the principles found in: 1 Corinthians 16:13; Ephesians 6:13-14; 2 Thessalonians 2:15; 1 Peter 5:12.

2. What does Proverbs 9:10 mean when it says, 'The fear of the Lord is the beginning of wisdom'?

3. 1 Corinthians 14:12 speaks about striving to build up the church. How can we do that?

A PRAYER

We pray to you, the Lord of the church, that as John Knox and others worked hard to reform the church according to the teaching of the Bible, your church today may continue to stand firm on these truths. Enable your people to demonstrate to the world the difference it makes for society as well as individuals to trust and follow Christ.

Making Progress
John Bunyan: Tinker, Prisoner and Best-selling Author

When you were younger, you probably heard and enjoyed the Mr Men/Little Miss stories.

Their creator, Roger Hargreaves, died some time ago, but his son has taken up the business and the series of stories has an abiding popularity, at least with young children. Last I knew, there were forty-six Mr Men and thirty-three Little Misses, and you'll remember the technique of having cartoon-type characters with names that tell of their character – Mr Greedy, Little Miss Bossy, Mr Topsy-Turvy and Little Miss Scatterbrain.

A similar thing was done by a writer who lived more than three hundred years ago. His name was John Bunyan and his most famous book, *The Pilgrim's Progress*, has proved to be one of the most popular books ever written. Only the Bible has sold more copies over the years than Bunyan's book, which has been published in dozens of different shapes and sizes.

Bunyan also created characters with descriptive names like Faithful, Hopeful and Charity on the one hand, and on the other hand Pliable, Lord Hategood and Giant Despair. There are also place-names with an obvious meaning, like Doubting Castle, Vanity Fair and Bypass Meadow.

Several things, however, make his story different from the Mr Men stories. One is the language he used, some of which seems rather old-fashioned nowadays and it's a good thing that the book has been published in several up-to-date versions. Another difference is in length – *Pilgrim's Progress* is considerably longer than any Mr Men story. Lastly, Bunyan's characters are meant to teach, not only good moral qualities, but sound biblical truth. On practically every page we find testimony to the author's knowledge of the Bible as well as his knowledge of human nature.

So who was this writer whose book sold 100,000 copies in its first year away back in the seventeenth century and was once read in many (possibly most) homes in our country?

John Bunyan was born in 1628 and lived to the age of sixty. He was born in the village of Elstow in Bedfordshire. His father was a tinker and made his living travelling from village to village mending pots and pans.

While John was still a boy, he gained the reputation of being 'a bit of a lad'. On one occasion, as he recounted later, he came upon an adder which he hit with a stick so that it was stunned, and then – 'I forced open its mouth with the stick and plucked its sting out with my fingers'![1]

He was foolhardy and, worse than that (in his own recollection): 'Even from a very young age, few could equal me for cursing, swearing, lying and blaspheming the holy name of God'.[2] As a teenager he made friends with others who shared in his misdeeds.

John became a tinker like his father, but when he was about sixteen he signed up as a soldier in the Parliamentary Army during the English Civil War. The Parliamentary Army was led

---

1. www.barnesandnoble.com/w/grace-abounding-to-the-chief-of-sinners-john-bunyan/1100171240 (Accessed 27.6.18).

2. Ibid.

by Oliver Cromwell and most of the soldiers were Puritans who sought to 'trust and obey' God (as a later hymn would express it). John was in the army for about three years, but the Christianity of his fellow-soldiers seemed to have little effect on him.

The person who did have some influence was his wife! Although we don't even know her name we do know that she was a godly woman and that she had a good influence on her husband. She sometimes read to him from devout books and she persuaded him to attend church with her.

One day the minister preached on the fourth commandment which is about keeping God's day holy. John wrote later of how he felt really guilty about the fact that, although he attended church, he spent the rest of Sunday in selfish pleasures and sports. However, as he recalled later, after he'd had a good lunch, such thoughts soon passed out of mind again! Perhaps he is not the only person to have had an experience like that.

Something had started in his heart and mind, however, and before long John was reading his Bible and seeking to live a different life; he even surprised himself when he realised that he had stopped swearing!

During his travels as a tinker, he sometimes went to Bedford and it was there that he came upon a group of women who were not merely 'religious' but who believed in the message of God's grace that saves the unworthy. It's the message found, among other places, in the third chapter of Romans:

> But now God has shown us a way to be made right with him without keeping the requirements of the law, as was promised in the writings of Moses and the prophets long ago. We are made right with God by placing our faith in Jesus Christ. And this is true for everyone who believes, no matter who we are. For everyone has sinned; we all fall short of God's glorious standard. Yet, God in his grace, freely makes us right in his

sight. He did this through Christ Jesus when he freed us from
the penalty for our sins. For God presented Jesus as the sacrifice
for sin. People are made right with God when they believe that
Jesus sacrificed his life, shedding his blood. This sacrifice shows
that God was being fair when he held back and did not punish
those who sinned in times past. (Romans 3:21-25 NLT)

The members of the church in Bedford introduced John to their
minister, the Reverend John Gifford, who, Bunyan learned, had
at one time been a gambler, drinker and blasphemer. Under
Gifford's influence, John came to accept Jesus into his heart; he
found, as Christian did in *The Pilgrim's Progress*, that his burden
fell off at the cross of Christ. He was a new man.

As time went by, he grew in his faith and he would sometimes
preach God's Word, in the church, in farm-buildings and even
the open-air.

In 1658 John's wife died after giving birth to their fourth
child, and John later married a woman called Elizabeth.

Trouble lay ahead, however, for Mr and Mrs Bunyan. After
the Restoration of the monarchy, people who did not share in
the worship of the established church were regarded as 'non-
conformists' and their meetings and services were declared to
be unlawful.

One Sunday in November 1660, as Bunyan was preaching in
a village, the police arrived to summon him to appear before the
Justice of the Peace on the following morning. For the 'crime'
of preaching the gospel of Christ, John was sentenced initially
to three months in Bedford prison. On several occasions he (or
Elizabeth on his behalf) was offered freedom on condition that
he would stop preaching, but he consistently refused, and he was
a prisoner for most of the next twelve years.

If someone had asked John whether it was all 'worth it' (one of the questions posed in the introduction to this book), he would certainly have said Yes. Faith did not give him an easy life – far from it – but he reckoned that faithfulness to his Saviour was worth it, whatever the consequences.

You could say he was like the apostle Paul who suffered much as a Christian (see 2 Corinthians 11:24-33); but he wrote, 'I count everything as loss because of the surpassing worth of knowing Christ Jesus my Lord. For his sake I have suffered the loss of all things and count them as rubbish, in order that I may gain Christ and be found in him.' (Philippians 3:8-9)

While in prison, John made shoelaces to support his family. He also wrote – and the authorities who jailed him could never have dreamt that, rather than silencing him, they were ensuring that Bunyan's name and influence would last for centuries through his most famous book, *The Pilgrim's Progress*.

Here are the opening sentences of the book (in the original style of English):

> As I walked through the wilderness of this world, I lighted on a certain place, where was a den (his prison); and laid me down in that place to sleep; and as I slept, I dreamed a dream. I dreamed, and behold I saw a man clothed with rags, standing in a certain place, with his face from his own house, a book in his hand, and a great burden upon his back.[3]

Of course, the book was the Bible, but Christian (the Pilgrim of the story) couldn't understand it. He needed a man called Evangelist to help him. Evangelist was probably modelled on the Reverend John Gifford who had helped John to grasp the Bible's message of salvation.

3. John Bunyan, *The Pilgrim's Progress* (London: Penguin Books edition, 1965 [originally published in 1678]), 39.

In the early part of the tale, Christian met Mr Worldly-Wiseman and then Pliable who would have turned him off the pathway altogether. Mr Worldly-Wiseman advised, 'In yonder village (the village is named Morality) there dwells a gentleman whose name is Legality'.[4]

This stands for human efforts to save ourselves by our own good deeds. It is the religion of many people. They suppose that doing good and religious things is the way to be accepted by God. The trouble is that, since God is perfect, we could never make ourselves good enough.

But Bunyan went on:

> Now I saw in my dream, that the highway up which Christian was to go, was fenced on either side with a Wall, and that Wall is called Salvation. Up this way therefore did burdened Christian run, but not without great difficulty, because of the load on his back.
>
> He ran thus till he came at a place somewhat ascending; and upon that place stood a Cross and a little below in the bottom, a sepulchre. So I saw in my dream, that just as Christian came up with the Cross, his burden loosed from off his shoulders, and fell from off his back; and began to tumble, and so continued to do till it came to the mouth of the sepulchre, where it fell in, and I saw it no more.
>
> Then was Christian glad and lightsome, and said with a merry heart, 'He hath given me rest, by his sorrow, and life by his death.'[5]

It is tempting to record more of the story, but if you want to read more, you'll need to get the book! More than three hundred years old as it is, it is still readily available in bookshops and libraries, either in its original form or in more modern language.

---

4. Ibid, 50.

5. Ibid, 69-70.

It goes on to tell of Christian's journey (his 'Progress') towards the heavenly city, passing many dangers along the way. For example, there were lions he encountered, but they were on chains and so long as he kept out of their reach he was safe. This was Bunyan's way of encouraging us to keep out of the devil's reach.

In another episode of the story, Christian was captured and thrown into a dungeon. He lay there for a while and then remembered that he had a key in his pocket that would open any door in Doubting Castle; it was a key called Promise. So Bunyan would teach us to rely on the promises God has given in His Word.

So it goes on, with meaning and significance all the way for those with eyes to see.

One of the most famous sections (though it is from the second part) is one which has been used as a hymn. Most modern hymnbooks put it in the form, 'He who would valiant be', but the original words are:

> Who would true valour see
> Let him come hither;
> One here will constant be,
> Come wind, come weather.
> There's no discouragement
> Shall make him once relent
> His first avowed intent
> To be a pilgrim.[6]

'To be a pilgrim' – that is a wonderful thing: to trust in Jesus as the Saviour who died that we might be forgiven, the Lord who wants to guide us through this life to the celestial city and the Friend who would be our unseen companion along the way.

Such encouragement is the legacy of John Bunyan, the Bedford tinker.

---

6. Ibid, 354-355.

TALKING POINTS

1. This chapter refers to Christian having a key that would open any door in Doubting Castle; the key was called Promise. Can you think of some of the promises God has given us in His Word?

2. Read for yourself the passage that affected John Bunyan very much: Romans 3:21-25.

3. Do you recognise John Bunyan's experience of being challenged by something you heard in church but you soon forgot all about it?

A PRAYER

Father, we thank you for stories that help us understand things about you and your gospel and especially for the influence that *Pilgrim's Progress* has had through the years. Help us to avoid all sidetracks and to progress along the road of discipleship, following Jesus as Saviour and Master.

Persevere
William Wilberforce: The Politician who Wouldn't Give Up

When Wikipedia says about William Wilberforce, 'He became an evangelical Christian, which resulted in major changes to his lifestyle and a lifelong concern for reform',[1] it gives an unintended answer to one of the questions raised at the start of this volume, namely, 'Does it matter?' Does a person's religious outlook make any difference to anything? Is it more significant than whether he loves or loathes golf or whether she is a jogger or a couch potato?

G. K. Chesterton once referred to the times when people fought fiercely over rival points of view. He wrote, 'It is foolish for a philosopher to set fire to another philosopher because they do not agree in their theory of the universe. This was done frequently in the Middle Ages and it failed altogether in its object.'[2] Nearly everyone would agree with that, but he went on, 'But there is one thing that is infinitely more absurd and unpractical than burning a man for his philosophy. This is the habit of saying that his philosophy does not matter.'[3]

---

1. www.alamy.com/stock-photo-william-wilberforce-1759-1833-was-an-english-politician-philanthropist-111456750.html (accessed 27.6.18).

2. Quoted by James S. Stewart, *River of Life* (London: Hodder & Stoughton, 1972), 72.

3. Ibid.

The life and achievements of William Wilberforce show that a person's beliefs certainly do matter. Some things are matters of little consequence (whether you prefer rap, pop or classical music, for example), but our basic beliefs make a huge difference to the lives we live and the influence we have on the world around us. It was his Christian convictions that led Wilberforce to campaign with great persistence for the abolition of the slave trade, the reform for which he is most remembered.

He was born in Hull on 24th August, 1759. He did not enjoy good health in his lifetime; as a child he was small and delicate, with poor eyesight, and in later years he would suffer a nervous breakdown in his mid-thirties.

A year after he started school (at the age of eight), his father died and when his mother struggled to cope he was sent to live with a wealthy aunt and uncle in London. They were devout Christians, but after a time William's mother was concerned that they were rather over-the-top in their zeal and she brought William back to Hull.

There his faith faltered and he entered into a more or less godless lifestyle, which continued when he became a student at Cambridge University. He and his friend, the future Prime Minister William Pitt, became playboys who indulged in gambling and late-night drinking sessions.

He had inherited money which made him wealthy and he was not too keen on the idea that students should actually study! Nevertheless he managed to graduate, but it was while he was still at university that he decided to stand as a candidate for parliament. He was only twenty-one and he was duly elected as the Member of Parliament for his hometown of Hull – at the time the youngest ever M.P.

A huge turning-point in his life came about in 1784 when he was on holiday in Europe with his mother, sister and Isaac

Milner (who was the brother of William's former headmaster). Milner's name is not well-known now but he had a large part to play, humanly speaking, in Wilberforce's Christian conversion. They studied the Bible together and William wrote that he felt he had been touched by 'the unspeakable mercies of my God and Saviour'.[4]

His whole outlook and value-system was changed at that time. He sobered up and devoted himself to the improvement of conditions for factory workers and then, most famously, to the campaign for the abolition of the slave trade.

His commitment to Christ and His Word led William to the conviction that human beings ought to be treated as human beings. Later in his life he arranged for the famous potter, Josiah Wedgwood, to create a brooch which featured a picture of a black man in chains with the caption, 'Am I not a man and a brother?'

Britain had been involved in the slave trade for a long time. The so-called 'triangular route' took British goods to Africa to buy slaves, then (in the 'middle passage') shipped the slaves to the West Indies and brought slave-grown products such as sugar, tobacco and cotton back to Britain. At the end of the eighteenth century, 40,000 slaves a year were taken from Africa on British ships and it has been estimated that eleven million Africans (that's about twice the present population of Scotland) were so transported over the years with nearly one and a half million dying during such voyages.

However, such bare statistics don't really convey the horror of what Wilberforce was determined to stop. What follows is a summary of a 1789 account written by a former slave, Olaudah Equiano from Nigeria. His support helped Wilberforce in his

---

4. http://www.reformationsa.org/index.php/history/145-william-wilberforce-set-ting-the-captives-free (accessed 27.6.18).

efforts and this summary gives a small taste of what the slave trade meant:

A ten-year-old boy from a wealthy family in Nigeria is playing with his sister. Suddenly two men climb over a wall into the garden and grab the children, covering their mouths before they can scream. They are tied up, gagged and carried off, the boy in a bag. Two days later the girl is sold, torn from her brother's arms as they sleep; then the boy too is sold and he changes hands several times before finding himself on a ship.

There he is met by the terrifying sight of countless chained men and he is shut up below deck with as many as can be chained shoulder to shoulder in the space. What strikes him most is the smell. Large conical tubs serve as toilets for all who can reach them – children often fall in – and for those who cannot there is the floor where they lie. The toxic stench is unbearable and before they have even set sail, Equiano falls ill. He feels too sick to eat but the sailors have the financial sense not to allow any slaves to starve themselves and they whip him until he eats.

Slaves take whatever opportunity arises on the journey to kill themselves. They are allowed on the top deck every day to get air and two slaves manage to jump into the sea and drown themselves; a third is retrieved and the sailors flog him severely 'for thus attempting to prefer death to slavery'.

The journey to Barbados takes a couple of months and from here Equiano is taken to North America where he is eventually sold for about £40 to an English naval officer. He survives, however, to publish his autobiography thirty-five years later, thus emerging into history out of all the unknown Africans who lost their freedom, their names, their families and, more often than not, their lives to put affordable sugar on to the tables of British homes.[5]

---

5. Summarised from account quoted in *William Wilberforce* by S. Tomkins (Oxford: Lion Hudson, 2007), 7f.

Such tales could be multiplied thousands of times, and it was this cruel trade that Wilberforce was determined to stop.

However, it could have been otherwise, because, after his conversion, he initially thought that his new faith would mean that he should give up the so-called 'dirty game' of politics, and it is one of the remarkable 'co-incidences' of history that the person who persuaded him otherwise was none other than the former slave ship captain, John Newton. He (and others) persuaded Wilberforce that he had a divine opportunity to work for change from within the political system. If he was concerned about the moral and spiritual state of the nation - which he was - he should use his political influence to serve Christ and his fellow-human beings.

In 1787 he came into contact with a group of anti-slave-trade activists, including Thomas Clarkson and Hannah More. His friend, William Pitt, by that time Prime Minister, also persuaded William to read a book that exposed the horrors of the slave trade, and these factors persuaded William to devote most of his energies to the abolition of this vile trade, despite many denials that there was a problem. Slave traders claimed that the reports of overcrowding, illness and animal-like treatment of slaves were wrong, with even the famous Admiral Nelson expressing hatred for the ideas of 'Wilberforce and his hypocritical allies'.[6]

However, it was one thing to take up the cause and another to carry it through to the end. In fact, it would be twenty years before parliament passed the Slave Trade Act in 1807. Despite William's eloquent speeches there was huge resistance and some of his supporters gave up the battle. It is likely that repeated defeats in parliament contributed to his poor health and nervous breakdown.

6. https://creation.com/anti-slavery-activist-william-wilberforce-christian-hero (accessed 27.6.18).

As a child I attended a primary school (Leith Academy) that had the single-word motto, 'Persevere'. That could have been Wilberforce's motto too. He must have had extraordinary resilience to carry on despite his Bill being defeated over and over again – something like twenty times.

At last, however, on 23rd February 1807 the House of Commons debated abolition and on this occasion speech after speech praised Wilberforce. Although applause is supposedly forbidden in the House, they gave him a standing ovation and voted 283 to 16 to abolish the slave trade.

The then Prime Minister, Lord Grenville, described Wilberforce's victory as 'a measure for which his memory will be blessed by millions yet unborn', and a historian called it 'one of the turning points in the history of the world.'[7]

The Act became law on 25th March that year, but Wilberforce was not finished yet. The slave *trade* had been abolished, but what about slavery itself? He continued to campaign until ill health forced him to resign from parliament in 1826 and it was in 1833 that the Slavery Abolition Act was passed. Wilberforce died three days later.

Anti-slavery was not Wilberforce's only interest. His faith led him to seek to honour the Lord in many other ways also. He supported missionary work overseas, he helped in the reform of the penal system and he also helped to found the British and Foreign Bible Society and the Royal Society for the Prevention of Cruelty to Animals. In 1824 he was one of the initial supporters of the founding of the National Institution for the Preservation of Life from Shipwreck (later re-named as The Royal National Lifeboat Institution which now operates 444 lifeboats and over

---

7. G. M. Trevelyan; quoted by Dennis Hill in 'William Wilberforce and the Abolition of the Slave Trade' in Evangelical Times, December 2017.

the years has saved 140,000 lives while losing 600 of its serving lifeboatmen).

And all of it was the outworking of his commitment to Jesus Christ. He wrote a book about it, which was reprinted five times within its first six months and translated into French, Italian, Dutch and German – not that it had a catchy title; it is sometimes known as 'Real Christianity' but its full title is: 'Practical View of the Prevailing Religious System of Professed Christians in the Higher and Middle Classes in this Country Contrasted with Real Christianity.' It was a best-seller for forty years and is said to be one of the longest titles to be found on Amazon!

He highlights the difference between a merely formal religion and real Christianity. The heart of real Christianity is a personal response to the message of God's grace. It involves repentance and asking for His forgiveness, accepting Christ as Saviour on the basis of what He did at Calvary, and commitment to Him as Lord and Master.

An old hymn has the chorus, 'Trust and obey'[8] – that's what real Christianity is about and it was that faith that made such a difference in William Wilberforce's life and, because of him, in the lives of so many other people.

Unfortunately there is a tendency today to want to re-write history and even write Christianity out of history. A sentence in the French magazine *Le Figaro* applies to the U.K. and most of western Europe: 'The secularist drive to rid France of its Christian past is becoming insane.'[9]

It is wrong-headed and dishonest to overlook the enormous benefits that have come through the influence of Jesus Christ. When people try to write Christianity out of history and write it off as far as modern relevance is concerned, they are – in

8. Hymn 'When we walk with the Lord' by John Henry Sammis, 1846-1919.

9. This was quoted in a Christmas letter from the Rev Bill Wallace, December 2017.

the familiar image – cutting off the branch on which they are sitting. Or, putting it differently, someone else has described the secularised society of most European counties today as 'like a vase of flowers, with each bloom now cut off from its Christian roots. It now appears that the petals are falling off the flowers.'[10]

Obviously many atheists and secularists lead good lives, but often that is the fruit of Christian influences from the distant or recent past. But if the roots are undermined, how long will the fruit last?

The abolition of slavery was not, of course, the end of all injustice or sin. It was one act in the constant battle against the effects of sin and selfishness – things like sexual slavery, racial prejudice, terrorist violence, theft, gang warfare, and so on. But there is a famous remark of G. K. Chesterton who was quoted at the beginning of this chapter. There had been a series of newspaper letters about what is wrong with the human race, and he contributed a letter to the editor that simply said, 'Dear Sir, I am, Yours sincerely, GKC'.[11] That's the problem, and it was when William Wilberforce responded to the wonderful grace of God that huge positive consequences followed.

His story shows that you don't need to have perfect health before you can make a difference in the world. He suffered constant ill health but he didn't allow it to hold him back. His story is also a remarkable example of perseverance despite many set-backs and much opposition.

And a present-day minister in Wilberforce's home city of Hull has suggested, 'The most fitting response we could make to Wilberforce's life would be to pick up a copy of the Bible that

10. Julia Doxat-Purser at meeting of the European Evangelical Alliance in February 2017; quoted in IDEA, May/June 2017.

11. Quoted in T. Keller, *The Prodigal God* (Dutton, 2008), 46.

he loved so much, read it and pray to the God that he adored, through His Son, Jesus Christ.'[12]

Whether we are parliamentarians or ordinary citizens, people with public influence or seemingly insignificant people, God's call for us is to trust in Him and to let our light shine for Him.

---

12. Dennis Hill, 'William Wilberforce and the Abolition of the Slave Trade'. *Evangelical Times,* December 2017.

TALKING POINTS

1. How does William Wilberforce's life show that Christianity makes a difference?

2. Look online for the Wedgwood brooch showing a black man in chains and the caption, 'Am I not a man and a brother?'

3. Isaiah 58 has much to say about practical Christian action. Consider how Wilberforce put verse 6 into action.

A PRAYER

We remember with thanksgiving the perseverance and commitment of Wilberforce and give thanks for all who have sought to live out their faith in Jesus by showing love to their fellow human beings, especially those in special need of help. May we do what we can to honour the Lord by seeking to make the world a better place.

'Dr Livingstone, I presume'
David Livingstone: Medical Missionary and Explorer

How would you have liked to be able to leave school when you were ten? You might have loved that – but not if you'd had to take a job where the working day lasted from six in the morning until eight at night and you had to work six days a week.

That was what faced young David Livingstone, the second of seven children in his family in Blantyre, Lanarkshire. He was born on 19th March 1813 and he started work in 1823 at a cotton mill, earning all of seven pence per day. It is difficult to know how that compares with monetary values today, but it wasn't a lot!

From an early age David was keen to learn and we are told that with his first week's wages he bought a Latin grammar book and then gave the rest to his mother!

He would take books to work and prop them up on the loom so that he could read while he worked, and for a time he attended a night school for two hours after the long working day. Then late at night he would read by candle-light until his mother remembered about him and came to blow out the candle!

After hearing stories about a missionary in China, he developed the thought that he too would like to be a missionary.

But how could someone from a poor family qualify for any profession (in days before education was free for all)?

However he did manage to save some money and eventually attended what is now Strathclyde University in Glasgow. In 1836, at the age of twenty-three, he qualified as a doctor of medicine and he wrote to the London Missionary Society about his sense of calling to go to China as a missionary doctor.

He also met a missionary called Robert Moffat who spoke about the vast continent of Africa where, Moffat said, he had seen the smoke of a thousand villages where no missionary had ever been. Circumstances made it impossible to go to China and David formed the ambition of going to Africa which was then hardly known to westerners.

Eventually, one day in November 1840, the Livingstone family rose at 5 am, read Psalm 121 and David left Blantyre for Glasgow to board a ship for Africa. The voyage would take him about three months.

That Psalm says that God does not slumber or sleep and that He will watch over His people (see verse 4). David would later say that he had found it to be true. He would also refer to Jesus' words at the very end of Matthew 28 – 'I am with you always' – as the words of a Gentleman who keeps His promises. He said that that promise sustained him through his many years of service.

In his early days in Africa, he started work at eight in the morning, teaching both adults and children to read and write. After lunch, he tended people who were ill and in the evening he would hold a service in the open air to tell people about Jesus.

Robert Moffat was mentioned earlier. He was a missionary among the Bechuana people at Kuruman and he and his wife had ten children, of whom the oldest was Mary. Mary was brought up on the mission station and eventually became a teacher in the school at Kuruman. It was there that she met David Livingstone. They fell in love and were married in January 1845, eventually having six children: Robert, Agnes, Thomas, Elizabeth, William and Anna.

One of the chiefs Livingstone met was called Sechele. He became a Christian through Livingstone's witness and he was very keen to learn. He had never seen a book before meeting Livingstone, yet he managed to learn the whole alphabet in a day. Later he became an effective missionary who possibly did more to spread the gospel in Africa than any European missionary.

I don't know whether you've heard the expression 'rice Christians'. It is sometimes used by cynics who allege that many 'converts' have professed Christianity for the material benefits they could obtain by doing so – rice in some countries, different things in other countries. In this country there may have been people who professed Christianity because it gave them social position or better job prospects. In the case of Sechele's motives, I once read the refreshing suggestion: 'The simplest explanation is the most obvious: he converted to Christianity because David Livingstone convinced him that it was true.'[1]

Mind you, he also had some slightly unorthodox ideas about how Livingstone should spread the gospel. If you were asked how that could be done, you might suggest praying for people, setting a good example for them and telling them about God's love. Chief Sechele suggested that David should whip them until they said they would worship Jesus! David didn't take his advice!

Besides working as a teacher, doctor and evangelist, David Livingstone was also an explorer. He travelled over much of southern and central Africa and 'discovered' places that western people hadn't known about previously. For example, he was the first European to see the falls known by an African name that means 'the smoke that thunders', which he named the Victoria Falls in honour of the Queen.

1. S. Tomkins, *David Livingstone – The Unexplored Story* (Oxford: Lion Hudson, 2013), 237.

Mary accompanied her husband on some of his explorations although on other occasions he would be away from the family for lengthy periods.

David was appalled to see a great amount of slave trading going on in Africa and he worked hard to stamp it out. Sometimes slaves were forced to wear wooden yokes and David would take a saw and literally cut the yokes from their necks.

This, of course, did not make him popular with slave-traders but he believed that no-one has a right to 'own' another human being. One example of the slave-traders' hatred was an occasion when David had written forty letters and paid carriers to take them to the coast, but servants of the slave-traders seized them and destroyed every one of them.

It was sixteen years before Livingstone made his first return to Great Britain and when he came back, it was to a hero's welcome. He received many honours, such as an honorary degree (Doctor of Laws) from Glasgow University. He also met Queen Victoria. She had the reputation of being very serious, but we're told that she laughed when Livingstone told her that he would tell African chiefs that he had met his own chief and that they would probably ask how many cows she had, since that was their gauge of wealth.

His return to Britain was also very emotional as his father had died just before David arrived. Although he must have been a pretty rugged individual, having faced lions and many other dangers in Africa, it's said that he wept when he saw his father's empty chair.

In 1858 he returned to Africa, although he was no longer serving under the auspices of the London Missionary Society; it seems that the Society felt he spent too much time in exploration. He was appointed Her Majesty's Consul for the East Coast of Africa and, as such, he continued his explorations, saying on one occasion, 'I am prepared to go anywhere – provided it be forward'.

It is reckoned that he covered about 30,000 miles in Africa. He talked about opening up a way for commerce and Christianity; the commerce would help the African people financially and the Christianity would be the principal means of doing away with the slave trade.

In April 1862 Mary became very ill with fever which led to her early death; she was only forty-one. Some people have suggested that David was not a very devoted husband, but a surviving welcome-home poem written by Mary in 1856 tells of a real bond of love and devotion between husband and wife. She wrote:

'A hundred thousand welcomes! How my heart is gushing o'er
With the love and joy and wonder thus to see your face once more.'

and for the future:

'And if death but kindly lead me to the blessed house on high,
What a hundred thousand welcomes will await you in the sky!'[2]

There is the expression of faith in the Bible's teaching that death is like falling asleep. In 1 Thessalonians 4:13, for example, Paul wrote, 'But we do not want you to be uninformed, brothers, about those who are asleep, that you may not grieve as others do who have no hope.' There is a natural sorrow when loved ones die but, as Paul went on to say in verse 14, 'Since we believe that Jesus died and rose again, even so, through Jesus, God will bring with him those who have fallen asleep.'

After Mary's death, David wrote to Thomas, one of their sons, expressing the Christian assurance that, although they had been parted for a time, they would be re-united in heaven.

David continued his work of healing, exploring and spreading the message of Jesus. He was, as we have seen, strong in his opposition to slavery. He once wrote a letter to the *New York Herald*, in which he said, 'All I can say in my loneliness is, may

---

2. https://en.wikisource.org/wiki/The_Personal_Life_Of_David_Livingstone/Chapter_X (accessed 5.6.18)

Heaven's rich blessing come down on every one who will help to heal this open sore of the world'.[3]

Eventually David himself became weak and ill.

In our modern world of e-mails, text-messages and other social media, we need to remember that in those days someone could be out of contact for very long periods. This is what happened to David; for something like six years there was no contact between him and the outside world, and that gave rise to what is one of the most famous stories about Livingstone (reflected in the title of this chapter).

The New York Herald commissioned a journalist called Henry Stanley to go to Africa and find Livingstone if he were still alive. Stanley told of how he asked the manager of *The Herald* how much money he could spend in the course of this expedition; the answer was: 'Draw £1,000 now, and when you have gone through that, draw another £1,000, and when that is spent, draw another £1,000, and when you have finished that, draw another £1,000, and so on — BUT FIND LIVINGSTONE!'[4]

Find him he eventually did, towards the end of 1871, at a place called Ujiji. Stanley wrote in his journal, 'As I advanced towards him I noticed he was pale, that he looked wearied and wan, that he had grey whiskers and a moustache, that he wore a bluish cloth cap'.[5]

Stanley approached him and said, 'Dr Livingstone, I presume?' It was a somewhat whimsical greeting since Livingstone was the only white man for miles around.

Livingstone enjoyed Stanley's company. Stanley had brought a bag of letters from home, the first David had received for years; those with signs of being from statesmen and scholars were overlooked as he eagerly read the letters from his children first.

---

3. Quoted by B. Matthews, *Livingstone – The Pathfinder* (Livingstone Prass, 1948), 117.

4. S. Tomkins, David Livingstone – The Unexplored Story (Oxford: Lion Hudson, 2013), 219.

5. Basil Mathews, *Livingstone, The Pathfinder* (Livingstone Press, 1948), 111-2.

Stanley was most impressed with the man he had been sent to find; he wrote in his journal that if he had been with Livingstone much longer, he would have been compelled to be a Christian, even though David hadn't tried to 'convert' him. It was the integrity and Christ-likeness of the man that impressed Stanley.

Stanley tried to persuade Livingstone to return to Britain for his health's sake, but David was adamant about remaining in his beloved Africa, and there he died at Ilala (in present-day Zambia) on 1st May 1873. His servants came in to his hut one day and found him kneeling at his bedside with his head buried in his hands. They thought he was praying but eventually realised that his life had ended. He had died in the attitude of prayer.

His body was brought back to Britain where it was buried in Westminster Abbey.

He had come a long way from his early home in Blantyre and that family reading of Psalm 121 with its assurance, 'The Lord watches over you'.

When he was given his honorary doctorate in Glasgow in 1856, his left arm hung by his side as the result of an encounter with a lion. But he asked the audience, 'Would you like me to tell you what supported me through all the years of exile among a people whose language I could not understand and whose attitude toward me was always uncertain and often hostile?'

He went on to answer his own question: 'It was this – 'And behold, I am with you always, to the end of the age' (Matthew 28:20). On these words I staked everything and they never failed'.[6]

---

6. Ibid, 83-84.

TALKING POINTS

1. Why was Matthew 28:19-20 so important to David Livingstone?

2. What do you think it was about Livingstone that made such an impression on Henry Stanley?

3. What answer do you think Livingstone would have given to our question, 'Is it worth it (to follow Jesus)?'

A PRAYER

Along with many people in Africa today, we give thanks for the memory of David Livingstone as one who wanted others to know about Jesus Christ, His great salvation and the difference it makes to trust and follow Him. Bless and help all missionaries today and may all your people be guided in seeking to spread the gospel.

To God be the Glory
Fanny Crosby: Blind Poet, Teacher and Hymn-writer

Eyesight is wonderful. We take it for granted, but a moment's thought would remind us of hundreds of things that would be much more difficult if we couldn't see. To lose one's sight must create many problems, but the person who is the subject of this chapter did not allow it to ruin her life. Having lost her sight in very early life, she wrote a little poem when she was eight years old:

> O what a happy child I am, although I cannot see!
> I am resolved that in this world contented I will be.
> How many blessings I enjoy that other people don't;
> So weep or sigh because I'm blind – I cannot and I won't.[1]

Her name is Fanny Crosby and, far from indulging in self-pity and allowing blindness to spoil her life, she became a teacher and she also wrote thousands of hymns, of which approximately sixty are still in use. If you have attended church for any length of time, it is quite possible that you have sung one or more of them, because they include such well-known hymns as 'To God be the glory', 'Blessed assurance' and 'Safe in the arms of Jesus'.

---

1. www. eaec.org/faithhallfame/fanny_crosby.htm (accessed 5.6.18).

Fanny was born in New York State in 1820 and she lived a long life, reaching the age of ninety-five; when she was eighty-three she said that she felt that she was in her prime!

But when she was only six weeks old, there was something wrong with her eyes and when she was taken to a doctor, the doctor made a dreadful mistake. He prescribed a kind of mustard poultice which did deal with the infection but left scars on her eyes that led to her being blind for life. We are told that the doctor concerned never got over it for the rest of his life.

A few months later, Fanny's dad became ill and died, and her mother, widowed at twenty-one, took employment as a maid while Fanny's granny took care of her. Granny became the little one's eyes and helped develop Fanny's descriptive abilities.

It was not a wonderful start to life, but Fanny was not given to self-pity; later she could write, 'I could climb a tree like a squirrel and ride a horse bareback'.[2] She had a very good memory; by the age of ten she had managed to learn the gospels of Matthew, Mark, Luke and John as well as other parts of the Bible. Towards the end of her long life, she would say, 'The Bible has nurtured my entire life.'[3]

At the age of eleven she entered the New York City Institution for the Blind and remained there for twenty-three years as a pupil and then teacher (of language and history). While a pupil she was apparently not keen on one particular subject and expressed that dislike in the little ditty: 'I loathe, abhor, it makes me sick to hear the word arithmetic'.[4]

In 1858 she married a blind musician, Alexander van Alstyne – she is sometimes known by her married name of Frances van Alstyne. He was a musician and Fanny herself played the guitar,

---

2. K. W. Osbeck, *101 More Hymn Stories* (Michigan: Kregel Publications, 1985), 239.

3. Ibid.

4. http://landmarksse.org/fannycrosby.html (accessed 27.6.18).

harp, piano and organ. She had a good singing voice also and even when she was an old lady, she would sit at the piano and sometimes even play old hymns in a jazzed up style.

It seems that she was no shrinking violet and the story is told of a time during the American Civil War when she displayed her northern patriotism by wearing a Union flag pinned to her blouse. One day in a restaurant, a lady from the southern states, the enemy at the time, said to her, 'Take that dirty rag away', and Fanny (who was less than five feet tall, weighed just over seven stones and was blind) responded, 'Repeat that remark at your own risk!'[5] The restaurant manager had to step in to defuse the situation!

However, she herself saw her particular mission in life as the writing of hymns. She also served in charitable and mission work, but it is for her hymns that she is most remembered. She has helped countless people to do what Ephesians 5:19-20 says Christians should do: 'Addressing one another in psalms and hymns and spiritual songs, singing and making melody to the Lord with your heart, giving thanks always and for everything to God the Father in the name of our Lord Jesus Christ.'

She wrote a huge number of hymns (some estimate about 8,000) and it is said that she would occasionally hear a hymn that sounded unfamiliar to her and on enquiring about the author, she would be told that it was one of her own!

Singing has always been an important part of the life of faith, whether we recall words like that of the Psalmist who said, 'He put a new song in my mouth, a song of praise to our God' (Psalm 40:3) or think of Paul and Silas singing at midnight even when unfairly imprisoned in Philippi (Acts 16:25). There are hundreds of references in the Bible to singing and at least fifty exhortations to sing.

---

5. www.christianity.com/church/church-history/timeline/1801-1900/fanny-crosby-americas-hymn-queen-11630385.html (accessed 27.6.18).

In the church we have a rich heritage in the psalms, hymns and songs that have been passed on to us, and also in the songs that are being written today. When Psalm 40 talks about a 'new song', it doesn't mean that there is no place for old songs; old and new together can give expression to the church's worship and fellowship.

More than a hundred years before Fanny Crosby was born, there was in Southampton, England a twenty-year-old youth called Isaac Watts who expressed dissatisfaction with the hymns that were sung in the church his family attended. He complained about them and his father challenged him, 'Well then, why don't you give us something better to sing?'

It was a challenge and possibly his father expected it to be forgotten, but Isaac rose to the challenge and wrote many 'new songs'. The first was based on words found in Revelation 5 and perhaps the third line was a bit of a dig at those who resisted the idea of writing new hymns:

> Behold the glories of the Lamb
> Amidst His Father's throne.
> Prepare new honours for His Name,
> And songs before unknown.[6]

He also wrote *Joy to the world*, and his *When I survey the wondrous cross* was so highly regarded by another famous hymn-writer, Charles Wesley, that he is reputed to have said that he would gladly have given up all of his own hymns to have written that one.

One of Fanny's enduring hymns is *Safe in the arms of Jesus*. It originated in a room in New York when she and a friend were joined by a Mr Doane who said he had composed a tune and wanted Fanny to write words for it. There was a small organ in the room and when Mr Doane played the tune, Fanny immediately

---

6. John Brownlie, *Hymns and Hymn Writers of the Church Hymnary* (London: Henry Frowde, 1911), 124.

said, 'That tune says "Safe in the arms of Jesus"; I will see what I can do.'[7] She went to another room and half an hour later came back with the now well-known hymn.

The phrase 'I will see what I can do' is interesting because when Fanny died in 1915 a tombstone was placed by her grave with the words of Mark 14:8 inscribed on it: 'She has done what she could'. Fanny probably would have been pleased with that, and what better thing could be said of anyone? God gives each of us the gifts we have and it is for us, in response to His amazing grace, to do what we can in the service of Christ and our fellow human beings.

In 1 Corinthians 12:17 Paul developed the picture of the human body with its varying limbs and organs which have their own parts to play in the life of the whole. He had a bit of fun with his idea of the foot complaining that it wasn't a hand and the ear wishing it were an eye. He asked, 'If the whole body were an eye, where would be the sense of hearing? If the whole body were an ear, where would be the sense of smell?' (verse 17)

In a similar passage in Romans 12:6-8 he spelt it out: 'Having gifts that differ according to the grace given to us, let us use them: if prophecy, in proportion to our faith; if service, in our serving; the one who teaches, in his teaching; the one who exhorts, in his exhortation; the one who contributes, in generosity; the one who leads, with zeal; the one who does acts of mercy, with cheerfulness.'

We are all different. God has given us different gifts and abilities, and our calling is to use whatever gifts He has given us, without envying others' gifts or wishing we were someone else. As the children's chorus says, 'Hallelujah, praise the Lord – right where we are'.

---

7. W. J. L. Sheppard, *Great Hymns and Their Stories* (Cambridge: Lutterworth Press, 1923), 80.

Many of Fanny Crosby's hymns are still sung as they were written, but in the case of *To God be the glory*, Nathan Fellingham has sought to re-invent it by setting it to a new tune, which has produced varying responses. One post on youtube says, 'I very much enjoy this new arrangement. It adds great life to the original words. It speaks to the new generation.'[8] A different post says, 'Beautiful hymn but that tune is just awful. Why not use the beautiful original by William Doane?'[9] You can't please all the people all the time! However, the great thing, as Fanny Crosby would say, is that we should sing praise to God. For one thing, if hymns and songs are based on sound biblical teaching, they can help us to grow in our faith and understanding of God's Word. In fact, it is sometimes said that most people who attend church learn more theology from the hymns sung than from the sermons preached. This is not tremendously encouraging to someone like me who has spent a lifetime preaching God's Word, but it is a reminder of the importance of the hymns we sing.

There are temptations for young teenagers to give up singing or to be less than half-hearted about it. This can be because you've outgrown the songs of Sunday Club and think singing is just for kids, or it may be because you've been scunnered by school choirs (or possibly rejected for the school choir). For boys there's the difficulty of coping when your voice seems to go all over the place and thinking that singing is just for girls.

But no such reasons are strong enough to justify us in failing to sing God's praise. People like Fanny Crosby (and others we've mentioned) have given us words, and I am sure she would have loved songs like the modern song (well, 2011 is reasonably modern) that says 'it's time to sing your song again':

---

8. www.youtube.com/watch?v=pJMM4uLPHmU

9. Ibid.

For all your goodness I will keep on singing;
Ten thousand reasons for my heart to find.
Bless the Lord, O my soul; O my soul, worship His holy name.
Sing like never before, O my soul, I'll worship Your holy name.[10]

Fanny Crosby would also have agreed with the last verse of that hymn by Matt Redman and Jonas Myrin, when it says:

And on that day when my strength is failing,
The end draws near and my time has come,
Still my soul will sing Your praise unending:
Ten thousand years and then for ever more![11]

She was undeterred by the loss of her eyesight. She even said, 'If I had a choice, I would still choose to remain blind … for when I die, the first face that shall ever gladden my sight will be that of my Saviour'.[12] That's something to sing about!

---

10. Hymn, "Bless the Lord, O my soul", by Jonas Myrin and Matt Redman (Thankyou Music, 2011).

11. Ibid.

12. http://www.azquotes.com/quote/1138994 (accessed 27.6.18).

TALKING POINTS

1.   How many hymns can you find (in hymn books or online) that Fanny Crosby wrote?

2.   Fanny learned to recite the whole of Matthew, Mark, Luke and John. Are there passages of Scripture that you can quote from memory?

3.   For an unusual setting for hymn-singing, look at Acts 16:25.

A PRAYER

Thank you, Lord God, that there are many hymns, psalms and spiritual songs, both old and new, that help us express our worship and praise. We give thanks for Fanny Crosby who overcame many obstacles in her life. Help us, whatever our situation, to honour you in body, mind and spirit and to use whatever gifts you have given us for the good of others and the praise of your name.

'She's Game, Boys'
Mary Slessor: Mill-girl to Missionary and Magistrate

The title of this chapter is the response made by some youths to Mary Slessor's unspoken 'I dare you'. They were members of a gang of youths who thought they'd have some fun at the expense of this redheaded mill-girl ('Carrots' to her brothers and sisters) who was on her way to a Christian meeting at which she helped to pass on to children the message of Jesus.

The gang had been throwing stones and bottles at the building and when Mary challenged them, they gathered round her and the gang leader started swinging a piece of rope round his head. It had a heavy weight attached at the end and as he kept swinging it round he let out a bit more of it each time so that it came nearer and nearer to Mary's face, eventually grazing her forehead. Would she back down and run away, leaving the gang to boast of their heroic exploits?

Presumably the gang members thought that's what would happen, but apparently they didn't really know Mary! She stood her ground, defying them to carry on, until they were the ones who had to back off, with that recognition, 'She's game, boys'.

In fact she persuaded them to come to the meeting where they too heard about Jesus, and many years later when Mary lived in Nigeria she had a photograph on her wall of a Christian man with his wife and family – the very gang leader who found that she wouldn't back down.

Mary was born in Aberdeen, the second of seven children. Sadly, her father, who was a shoemaker, was more interested in frequenting drinking dens than being a good father. Through alcohol he lost his job and when Mary was ten years old the family moved to Dundee where they found accommodation in a slum area of the city.

Mr Slessor's behaviour, however, was no better than it had been in Aberdeen and sometimes Mary would trudge the streets at night looking for her drunk father to bring him home quietly and save the family from public disgrace.

Many of us learned at school that Dundee was famous for its three Js - jute, jam and journalism - and it was in Baxter's jute mill that Mary began work.

At that time (Mary had been born in 1848) attendance at school was not compulsory (not till the Education Act of 1872) and, like many other ten and eleven year olds in Dundee, Mary started working as a 'half-timer'. Half-timers worked in the factory from 6 to 11 am and then attended school from noon to 6 pm. Then when she was fourteen, Mary became a full-time mill worker (6 am to 6 pm) and, even after such a long working day she would attend classes at night school.

The development of the jute industry, along with shipbuilding and whaling, led to a vast increase in the population of Dundee (from 26,000 to 166,000 within forty years), but housing and sanitation couldn't keep pace and many working class families, including the Slessors, ended up living in overcrowded slum areas with little or no sanitation. There was poverty, hunger, squalor and a short life expectancy.

Jute was imported from India and used for the manufacture of such things as sacks, rope and sail cloth, but work in the jute factories (of which there were about a hundred in Dundee) was noisy, smelly and dirty. By modern standards it would be totally unacceptable.

Mary attended Wishart Church in Dundee, in a building sometimes known as 'Heaven and Hell' because there was a pub on the ground floor and the church was upstairs on the first storey. Her mother was a committed Christian who already had a great interest in the United Presbyterian Church's mission in Calabar, Nigeria, and the more Mary heard about it, the more sure she became that her calling was to go there as a missionary.

This book is about people worthy to be regarded as heroes and it's interesting to know that Mary herself had a hero, namely David Livingstone. Her mother had read tales of Livingstone to Mary from the monthly U.P. Missionary Record.

After her father died, Mary was the financial mainstay of the family and she started working two looms in the factory instead of only one, but she still managed to find time to study her books and her Bible.

Eventually she offered her services to the Missions Board of the United Presbyterian Church and, after attending college in Edinburgh for three months, she was accepted as a teacher and assigned to Calabar.

So at the age of twenty-eight she set sail from Liverpool on the journey to Nigeria where she served for 38 years until her death in 1915, eventually being known as the White Queen of Okoyong, Okoyong being the name of the tribe among whom she spent many years.

The mission at Calabar had been established in 1846 and when Mary arrived it was a thriving place with many missionaries and other staff. She set to work immediately, teaching and also working in the dispensary. She learned the local language so that she could communicate better with the local people.

She was not keen on bureaucracy and had an 'interesting' relationship with the church authorities at home. She was unorthodox in many of her ways; for example, she abandoned the traditional female missionary attire – blouse and long skirt with gloves and a sun helmet – choosing instead to wear functional clothes like a light cotton dress, either canvas shoes or no shoes at all and no hat.

She ate local food (mainly vegetarian) rather than do what many other missionaries did, having supplies transported from Britain. Unlike most missionaries at the time, she deliberately sought to live like an African, living in huts like theirs and, when eventually considering church buildings she opposed the idea of building western-style churches – since she thought that would give the impression that Christianity was a foreign religion.

Life in Calabar then was grim. There was witchcraft. There was violence and terrorism. Criminal guilt was decided by poison ordeal in which the accused was made to drink a concoction made from a poisonous bean – if they vomited it up they were declared innocent; if they died, they must have been guilty!

When twins were born, it was believed that one of the babies was demon-possessed and since they couldn't tell which they killed both and banished the mother.

It was also a place where disease was rife; Mary herself had several bouts with malaria, and the country was known as 'the white man's grave'.[1] But she was undaunted. She prayed, 'Lord, the work is impossible for me but not for You; lead the way and I will follow.'[2]

---

1. Often-quoted phrase, found among other places in the Programme of Events at Mary Slessor Centenary, published in 2015 by the Mary Slessor Foundation, Dundee.

2. http://www.azquotes.com/author/23682-Mary_Slessor (accessed 27.6.18).

As mentioned, she worked as a teacher and before she died she had established about fifty elementary schools in various places with an estimated 2,000 pupils attending.

She visited people in their homes and she would often take in abandoned children, including twins who had escaped early infanticide. Altogether she adopted six girls and two boys as her own. The first of these was Janie whose twin had been killed. Missionaries were not encouraged by the mission societies to adopt them into their own families, but Mary, as we've seen, was not noted for her love of officialdom and she simply ignored this rule.

After three years in Calabar, Mary came home on furlough (leave). Sixteen months later she returned and after another three years came home again and looked after her mother and sister. Her third mission lasted for fifteen years, in which she moved to the Okoyong district, an area where white male missionaries had been killed previously.

The Okoyong had been a fierce and war-loving people who, it was said, even sat down to their meals with guns at the ready. Yet Mary settled there and gradually came to be respected, for all her smallness, as a settler of disputes. Even powerful and savage chiefs came to honour her and made her a trusted arbiter in all kinds of disputes, such as cases of land dispute, debt, defamation of character, wife-stealing and adultery. So much was this so that eventually she was appointed by the United Kingdom government as a magistrate – the first woman ever to be appointed to such a position.

The strength of her personality was demonstrated in a particular incident which bore a remarkable resemblance to the Dundee incident with the gang members. A woman had been accused of adultery and she was to be punished by having boiling water poured over her. Mary, however, pushed through the crowd and stood defiantly in front of the woman, while one of the men started swinging a long-handled ladle round his head and moved towards Mary. The weight came nearer and nearer to her head but she stood her ground and, to the amazement of everyone, the man backed off. Such power – and from a woman who was only five feet two inches tall!

Mary gradually persuaded people to stop the practice of killing twin babies; a 1907 government report recognised her work in this area, referring to the influence of 'that admirable lady, Miss Slessor'.[3] One website, which is now unobtainable, quoted an African as saying that all twins in Nigeria and Africa should honour and celebrate Mary Slessor, as she is the reason why they exist!

As Mary served God and the people among whom she lived, many lives were changed. She said that at first people would enjoy hearing the gospel; they would pray and clap their hands – and then go back to their old ways! But gradually her witness bore fruit and it was seen clearly in the changed lives of the people. Over time there was less plundering and stealing of slaves as the gospel of Christ was changing lives.

Our three questions about Christianity - is it true, does it work and is it worth it? – are all answered in the life and witness of Mary Slessor, and especially the second: does it work? The Bible says, 'If anyone is in Christ, he is a new creation' (2 Corinthians 5:17) and it gives us Jesus' Word, 'You will recognize them by their fruits' (Matthew 7:16). He asked, perhaps with a twinkle in His eye, 'Are grapes gathered from thorn bushes?'

And shortly after that He gave His famous parable of the two foundations. He spoke about the wise man and the foolish man. What was the difference? 'Everyone then who hears these words of mine and does them will be like a wise man who built his house on the rock' and conversely, 'Everyone who hears these words of mine and does not do them will be like a foolish man who built his house on the

---

3. W. P. Livingstone, *Mary Slessor of Calabar* (London: Hodder & Stoughton, 1915 edition), 233.

sand' (Matthew 7:26-27). And we all know what happened – what happens – when the rains come down and the floods come up.

It is not the doing of good deeds that brings us forgiveness and salvation, but those who have appreciated and received Christ's salvation will show it in the lives they live.

So it was in Nigeria as lives were changed through the influence for Christ of Mary Slessor whose difficult early life perhaps prepared the way for her steadfastness through the many dangers, toils and snares that she met in her life.

She was not perfect and did not claim great things for herself; she could be stubborn and obstinate, and when in 1913 she was to be awarded a medal in recognition of her services in the cause of humanity, she wrote, 'I never felt more unworthy or more small in my own respect than when I was singled out from others who are and have been working with far better results than mine.'[4]

To herself she was 'just an insignificant, wee auld wifey',[5] but on the occasion of the centenary of Mary's birth, a minister called Dr George Gunn remarked on the fact that Scotland had given nearly 300 missionaries to Calabar alone and described Mary as 'one of the most remarkable missionaries of all time'.

Yet, when she was awarded the distinction of receiving the medal of the Order of the Hospital of St John of Jerusalem, she said, 'Don't think that there is any difference in my designation. I am Mary Mitchell Slessor, nothing more and other than the unworthy, unprofitable, but most willing, servant of the King of kings.'[6]

---

4. Letter quoted in: McLennan, *Mary Slessor – A Life on the Altar for God* (Tain: Christian Focus 2014), 136.

5. W. Steven, *Heroes of the Faith* (Church of Scotland Youth Committee, 1952), 140.

6. W. P. Livingstone, *Mary Slessor of Calabar* (London: Hodder & Stoughton, 1915), 307.

TALKING POINTS

1. What difference did Mary Slessor's Christian commitment make for people in and around Calabar?

2. What does Romans 10:9 say about what it means to be a Christian?

3. Look at the successive steps of Paul's argument in Romans 10:13-15.

A PRAYER

Heavenly Father, we thank you for the example of perseverance and inner strength that we see in Mary Slessor and for the difference she made to so many people in Nigeria. Bless Christians in that country today, especially those who are under pressure because of their faith in Christ and send down your strength wherever people are persecuted for Christ's sake.

The Secret Room
Corrie ten Boom: Watchmaker and Protector of Nazi Victims

'How old do you have to be to …?' is a question that many teenagers ask at some stage. How old does one have to be to vote, to become a blood donor, to buy fireworks, to get married; in earlier years it might have been, 'How old do I have to be to go to school' – now, 'How old do I have to be to leave school'!

Here's another question: at what age can people trust in Jesus as their Saviour? Do you think five is too young? Well, it isn't according to the subject of this chapter – the remarkable Dutch lady called Corrie ten Boom. From an early age she loved stories, especially those about Jesus – Jesus who, she said, was a member of the ten Boom family and to whom it was just as easy to talk as it was to carry on a conversation with her mother and father, her aunts or her brother and sisters. From early in her life she trusted in Jesus.

Of course it was a faith that would develop and grow over the years – she lived to the age of ninety-one. Sadly, some people drop out of Christian involvement because they never advance beyond the simple faith they had as children – like the boy who explained why he had fallen out of bed one night by saying, 'I must have fallen asleep too near where I got in'!

Our understanding of the Bible and of salvation is meant to grow as we develop, but it is also wonderfully true that it's never too soon (or too late, for that matter) to put your trust in Jesus and begin to follow Him.

There's a text in the Bible that bids us remember our Creator; when? It says, 'Remember also your Creator in the days of your youth' (Ecclesiastes 12:1) – like Timothy who from childhood knew the Bible (2 Timothy 3:15) and Isaiah who wrote about the Lord who 'formed me from the womb to be his servant' (Isaiah 49:5).

The evangelist, D. L. Moody, said that at one of his missions there were seventeen and a half converts. People assumed that he meant seventeen adults and one child, but he explained that, on the contrary, he meant seventeen children who could give their whole lives to Christ and one adult who had already lived half of this life.

Corrie ten Boom gave the whole of her life to the service of Christ. She was born in Haarlem in 1892 and had a happy life as a child in the narrow three-storey house where her father worked on the ground floor as a watchmaker. She was not a brilliant student (she once said that Mischief was her middle name, or should have been) and, after leaving school at seventeen, she worked for a short time as an *au pair* but then came home to assist her aunt in house-keeping, cooking, cleaning and nursing.

Her sister Betsie worked as a book-keeper with their father in the shop, although later she and Corrie swapped roles and Corrie asked her father to teach her the trade of watch-making. She became the first woman to be licensed as a watchmaker in Holland.

Besides work, she established a youth club for girls. Sunday School classes ended when people were twelve or thirteen, and YWCA groups (Young Women's Christian Association) were designed at the time for girls of eighteen plus. Corrie saw that there was nothing much organised for the formative years in between, and this led her to develop a network of Friends' Clubs and eventually the Netherlands Girls Club which ran for twenty-five years until the outbreak of the Second World War. As well as classes in handicrafts, sewing and drama, the clubs provided religious instruction.

It was after that time, however, that her life, like that of so many people, took an unexpected turn. The story is told in her best-selling book, 'The Hiding Place', which tells of how she and her family saved the lives of hundreds of Jews during that Second World War when the Nazis, among other things, killed about six million Jews in the horrors of the concentration camps and gas chambers of places like Auschwitz, Treblinka, Belsen and Ravensbruck.

The cover blurb of the book describes it as a best-seller for more than four decades and as 'one of the greatest Christian testimonies of our time.'[1]

The ten Boom family lived happily in the house in Barteljorisstraat, known as the Beje. It was a devout family and extremely hospitable; many missionary kids and other homeless people were given accommodation.

This was the prelude to the use of the house as a hiding place after the German invasion and occupation of Holland during the war. Holland experienced the first large-scale airborne attack in the history of warfare. Germany demanded surrender, but even while the surrender negotiations were under way, bombers appeared and wiped out the heart of Rotterdam.

The army surrendered, Queen Wilhelmina fled and the German army marched through the streets – tanks, cannons, cavalry and hundreds of soldiers. Interestingly, the street in which the watch shop was situated, Barteljorisstraat, now features in

---

1. *The Hiding Place* by Corrie ten Boom with John and Elizabeth Sherrill (London: Hodder & Stoughton, 1971).

the Dutch version of Monopoly, but what happened then was no happy table game.

The ten Boom family, having already been in the habit of offering hospitality to many, now had a special concern for the Jewish community which was being hounded by the Nazis. By the time they were betrayed, they had saved the lives of about 800 Jews.

Inside Corrie's bedroom a false wall was built to form a secret room – the hiding place. Up to six people could clamber through a sliding panel in a bookcase and hide – the opening measured two feet by two feet.

When it was clear that there was going to be a spot search, one of the household would sound a buzzer, and a system was developed that enabled the refugees to get into hiding in just over one minute.

Some fugitives would stay in the hiding place for only a few hours while others would stay for several days until another 'safe house' could be located. Corrie became a leader in the 'Beje' movement, overseeing a network of 'safe houses' in the country.

She later described their activities: 'Ostensibly we were still an elderly watchmaker living with his two spinster daughters above his tiny shop. In actuality the Beje was the centre of an underground ring that spread now to the farthest corners of Holland. Here daily came dozens of workers, reports, appeals. Sooner or later we were going to make a mistake.'[2]

It was incredibly risky work, but all in the family were determined to save the lives of as many Jews as possible, whatever it would take.

There were many false alarms, but then on 28th February 1944 the Nazis, acting on the tip-off of a Dutch traitor, raided the house and took away thirty-five people, including Corrie, Betsie and their father.

2. Ibid, 106.

Corrie had flu at the time, which later developed into pleurisy, but she and her sister were beaten by the soldiers who wanted to know about any people in hiding. They searched the house but couldn't find the hiding place and it was later discovered that six Jews remained in the cramped space for three more days before being rescued by the Dutch underground.

Corrie's story is a story of immense courage. In answer to our question, 'Was it worth it?' – well, about 800 Jews were saved from arrest and death, even though the cost was very great for the ten Boom family.

Corrie, Betsie and their father Casper were taken first to a prison in Scheveningen near The Hague, where eighty-four year old Casper, 'Haarlem's Grand Old Man', died.

The two sisters were taken to another prison where they were treated as slaves and forced to work in factory conditions for thirteen hours a day. Sometimes they would hear gunshots from the nearby male prison; on one such occasion, they learned, 700 men were shot.

After some months they and many others were jammed into railway trucks which trundled along for two days and nights until they came to Ravensbruck concentration camp, near Berlin, which Corrie described as a city of low grey barracks surrounded by concrete walls and guard towers, with a huge chimney in the centre. They were kept in the open air for several nights before being paraded naked through a processing centre and assigned to their barracks – prisoners 66729 and 66730.

The treatment was terrible and the conditions were appalling. 1,400 prisoners were crammed into barracks intended for 400, with eight acrid and overflowing toilets; to reach them people had to crawl over bed-mates at the risk of breaking the sagging wooden slats on which they were supposed to sleep and crashing down on those below. For lunch they were given one potato and some thin soup and in the evening one piece of black bread and turnip soup.

Corrie had managed to smuggle a Bible in with her and she and Betsie held Bible study meetings in these most awful of conditions. On one occasion Betsie quoted the Bible text about giving thanks in all circumstances (1 Thessalonians 5:18); she would even give thanks for the crowded situation since that would allow more people to hear - and even for the fleas that infested the place. Corrie said there was no way she would give thanks for fleas, but it turned out that the guards tended to leave them alone as they didn't want to be infected!

Roll call for the tens of thousands of prisoners took place at 4.30 am and the prisoners were sent to forced labour for eleven hours a day. Betsie's health grew steadily worse and it was not long before her death that she spoke her now famous words to Corrie about what they should do if and when the ordeal was over: 'We must tell people what we have learned here. We must tell them that there is no pit so deep that He is not deeper still. They will listen to us, Corrie, because we have been here.'[3]

Betsie died on 16th December 1944 and it was left to Corrie to tell the tale.

Twelve days after her sister's death, for unexplained reasons, Corrie was released – a week before all women prisoners of her age were executed. She was sent to the hospital ward for a time, as people could only be released 'in good condition', but even there, she wrote, the suffering was unimaginable – women horribly mutilated and in terrible pain, with the nurses jeering callously and mimicking their groans.

But Corrie was released and eventually returned to Holland where she set up a post-war rehabilitation centre for survivors of the horrors of that terrible time. A wealthy lady made her fifty-six room mansion available as a centre. Corrie said that even more difficult than caring for their former tormentors was forgiving

3. Ibid, 202.

and accepting fellow Dutch people who had collaborated with the Germans during the occupation of the country.

She travelled widely, visiting more than sixty countries – including Germany, the one country in the world to which she had never wanted to return. When she left Ravensbruck she said to herself, 'I'll go anywhere God sends me, but I hope never to Germany'. But she did and she told of one amazing encounter.

She was speaking at a church service in Munich and as people were leaving a man thanked her for her message – he was grateful for it and how wonderful it was, he said, that Jesus had 'washed my sins away'. Corrie recognised the man; it was a former S.S. jailer who had stood guard at the shower room in Ravensbruck.

Suddenly it all came back to Corrie – the horror, brutality and inhumanity of their treatment there – and, as the man held out his hand to Corrie, she struggled with the situation – until 'the most incredible thing happened. From my shoulder along my arm and through my hand a current seemed to pass from me to him, while into my heart sprang a love for this stranger that almost overwhelmed me.'

She went on, 'So I discovered that it is not on our forgiveness any more than on our goodness that the world's healing hinges, but on His. When He tells us to love our enemies, He gives, along with the command, the love itself.'[4]

In 1977, when she was eighty-five, Corrie moved to California but a year later she suffered a series of strokes which left her unable to speak. She died five years later – on her birthday, 15th April, 1983.

Her story is an amazing story of survival, courage and complete dedication to doing the will of her Saviour. She showed love and forgiveness even in horrific times – proof that Christianity does indeed work, and make a difference!

---

4. Ibid, 220-221.

TALKING POINTS

1. At what age can people put their trust in Jesus?

2. What blessings did Paul say Timothy had in 2 Timothy 1:5 and 2 Timothy 3:15?

3. How would the ten Boom family have answered anyone who said their actions were courageous but misguided and were proved to be not 'worth it'?

A PRAYER

Lord, we thank you that even in the midst of the horrors of the Nazi era, the light of Christ shone in the lives of people like Corrie, Betsie and their family. Please save people from such maltreatment and wickedness. We pray in the words of Jesus, 'Your kingdom come, your will be done on earth as it is heaven.'

Behind the Wardrobe
C. S. Lewis: Scholar and Best-selling Author

Peter, Susan, Edmund and Lucy had been sent away from London during the air-raids of the Second World War. For their safety, they were sent to the house of an old professor who lived ten miles from the nearest railway station and two miles from the nearest post office. It was a large rambling house with many rooms to explore and on their first full day – when it was raining outside – they did just that.

> 'They looked into a room that was quite empty except for one big wardrobe; the sort that has a looking-glass in the door. There was nothing else in the room at all except a dead blue-bottle on the window-sill.
>
> 'Nothing there!' said Peter, and they all trooped out again – all except Lucy. She stayed behind because she thought it would be worthwhile trying the door of the wardrobe, even though she felt almost sure that it would be locked. To her surprise it opened quite easily …'[1]

So began the adventure – an adventure that would involve talking beavers, a white witch, Turkish Delight – and, of course, Aslan

---

1. C. S. Lewis and Pauline Baynes, *The Complete Chronicles of Narnia* (New York: Harper Collins edition, 1998), 77.

- 'a lion – the Lion, the great Lion'. When Lucy asks if he's safe, Mr Beaver famously says, ''Course he isn't safe. But he's good. He's the King, I tell you'.[2]

The lion clearly represents Jesus, and in his imaginative story the author, C. S. Lewis, goes on to give a picture of Jesus' coming into the world, His life, death and resurrection from the dead. It's told very differently from the way Matthew, Mark, Luke and John tell the story, but it's the same story, and Lewis invites us, in a different sense, to enter into the world beyond the wardrobe. In other words, he wants us to see that there is more to life than just the physical things of everyday.

He clearly had a very vivid imagination, although even he could never have imagined that his stories, especially his children's books such as *The Lion, The Witch And The Wardrobe,* would become as popular as they are. And as for big screen epics such as *Prince Caspian* and *The Voyage of the Dawn Treader* – they would have been beyond even the wildest of his dreams.

C. S. Lewis did a great deal to commend Christianity, but there was a period in his life when, if anyone had hinted that he would become a famous Christian writer, he would have said, 'No way!' (although he might have had a more eloquent way of saying it!) He had been an atheist and when he came to believe in God he described himself as a 'reluctant convert'.

It was when he was about thirty that he (as he put it himself) 'gave in and admitted that God was God, and knelt and prayed: perhaps that night, the most dejected and reluctant convert in all England'.[3]

Why so reluctant? It's not that he hadn't heard of God before. In fact he had been brought up with a kind of formal churchiness that was meant to lead him to trust in Jesus but somehow had

2. Ibid, 99.

3. C. S. Lewis, *Surprised by Joy* (New York: HarperCollins, 2002), 182.

the opposite effect, and for a long time he would have described himself as an atheist who had no time for religious mumbo-jumbo.

He was born in Belfast in 1898 and was educated at home by a governess and then sent to a boarding school in England. This was after the early death of his mother, which saddened the young Jack very much (he was known for most of his life by the name Jack rather than his given name of Clive); he wrote later 'With my mother's death all settled happiness disappeared from my life'.

He didn't like Malvern, the boarding school to which he had been sent, and eventually his father agreed to him having a tutor, a Mr Kirkpatrick (who had already tutored Jack's older brother, Warnie).

Mr Kirkpatrick seems to have been an inspiring teacher and eventually Jack became a student at Oxford University, where he excelled. He was appointed a Fellow of Magdalen College where he taught for thirty years until 1954 when he became Professor of Mediaeval and Renaissance Literature at Cambridge University. Such was his academic career.

Many people who become Christians would say that they were influenced in that direction by other people, and so it was with Jack. He had friends who believed in God, and gradually Jack came to this point when he 'gave in' and admitted in his heart that there must be a God.

However, as he said later, this was not the same thing as becoming a Christian, and it was not until a couple of years later that he put his trust in Jesus. In his *Surprised by Joy* he wrote about a journey to Whipsnade Zoo in Bedfordshire: 'When we set out I did not believe that Jesus Christ is the Son of God, and when we reached the zoo I did'.[4]

---

4. Ibid, 189.

That might sound like a sudden change of heart and mind, but he went on to say that he hadn't felt any great surge of emotion; in fact, 'It was more like when a man, after long sleep, still lying motionless in bed, becomes aware that he is awake'.[5]

It's a helpful picture, especially for others who may worry about not being able to refer to a definite point in time when they put their trust in Jesus. If you've been brought up to believe in God and be part of the church, you might sometimes almost envy people who've had a sudden or dramatic conversion. You might even wonder if the lack of such a sudden conversion means that you can't really be a Christian at all.

But think of how you sometimes need to get up at a certain time in the morning and so you set your alarm clock; as a result, you would be able to tell anyone who asked that you were awakened at (say) 7.30 am – not 7.20 or 7.35. There are other times, perhaps during the holidays, when you simply wake up when you wake up (in time for lunch?), and you probably couldn't say exactly when it was that you woke up. But the point is - you know you are awake!

Jack had woken up – woken up to the reality of Jesus Christ as a Saviour and Master who calls people to put their trust in Him and live under His authority. And after this time Jack – C. S. Lewis – became a very influential witness for Christ, helping many others to also wake up. He did not become a Christian because he found Christianity to be a nice story but because he had become convinced that the Christianity of the Bible is simply true.

His influence has been enormous, despite the fact that most of us might have found him slightly stuffy, the kind of person who would have no interest in wearing designer clothes (if they had been invented in his lifetime) and who probably wasn't in

5. Ibid.

any sense 'cool'. Yet his books are still being republished today – books like *Mere Christianity, Miracles, The Problem of Pain, The Screwtape Letters,* and so on.

Through his writing, he has strengthened many, especially against the snide remarks of some critics of 'religion' who imply that in order to be a Christian you have to leave your brains outside the room! You may find some of his books could strengthen your faith too.

He once remarked that a children's story which is enjoyed only by children is a bad children's story, and for many people C. S. Lewis is best-known as the author of the seven stories (published one a year from 1950 to 1956) about Narnia. *The Lion, The Witch And The Wardrobe* has been many people's first introduction to his books, enjoyable simply as a good story but also full of deeper meaning.

For example, it's not difficult to know what lies behind that part of the story where Aslan has been captured by the White Witch and it says:

> 'Others – evil dwarfs and apes – rushed in to help them. And between them they rolled the huge Lion over on his back and tied all his four paws together, shouting and cheering as if they had done something brave, though, had the Lion chosen, one of those paws could have been the death of them all'.[6]

It's like what we read about the arrest and mistreatment of Jesus in John 19:10-11.

And what about the part where Lucy and Susan were talking sadly about Aslan's death and then –

6. C. S. Lewis and Pauline Baynes, *The Complete Chronicles of Narnia* (New York: HarperCollins edition, 1998), 121-122.

'They looked round. There, shining in the sunrise, larger than they had seen him before, shaking his mane (for it had apparently grown again) stood Aslan himself.[7]

"Oh, Aslan!' cried both the children, staring up at him, almost as much frightened as they were glad.

"Aren't you dead then, dear Aslan?' said Lucy.

"Not now', said Aslan.

"You're not – not a – ?' asked Susan in a shaky voice. She couldn't bring herself to say the word ghost. Aslan stooped his golden head and licked her forehead. The warmth of his breath and a rich sort of smell that seemed to hang about his hair came all over her.

"Do I look it?' he said.

"Oh, you're real, you're real! Oh, Aslan!' cried Lucy.'[8]

There's one other section I would quote, this time from Prince Caspian. The story tells of Lucy meeting Aslan:

"Welcome, child', he said.

"Aslan', said Lucy, 'you're bigger'.

"That is because you are older, little one', answered he.

"Not because you are?'

"I am not. But every year you grow, you will find me bigger'.'[9]

The second letter of Peter ends with, 'Grow in the grace and knowledge of our Lord and Saviour Jesus Christ'(v. 18). Growth is important in all sorts of ways, and growing up in today's world faces young people with some difficult choices. The most important thing of all is to grow in grace and in faith as disciples of Jesus.

---

7. Ibid, 125

8. Ibid, 125.

9. Ibid, 259.

Jack continued with his other academic writing, and it was while he was working on English Literature in the Sixteenth Century that he became acquainted with an American lady who wrote him a letter. The lady, who was considerably younger than he was, was Joy Gresham.

One of Jack's books is called *Surprised by Joy*; it was true for him in more ways than one. 'Joy' for him wasn't joviality or cheerfulness, but rather the sense of inner peace that comes from being at one with oneself and at one with God. It was in Christ that Jack found such a sense of fulfilment and contentment.

But in another sense he was surprised by Joy, as he came to care more and more for this lady. She was separated from her husband who eventually wanted a divorce so that he could marry someone else.

Joy wanted to remain in England and, to help her out, Jack agreed to marry her - probably not the kind of marriage your parents would want for you! It was a marriage of convenience, since this was the means by which Joy could legally become a British citizen. Most people think in terms of falling in love and then marrying; Jack never was a slave to fashion and in his case the marriage came first and the falling-in-love later.

They were married in 1956 - and then the following year it was discovered that Joy had cancer. By then Jack had truly fallen in love with her and he was distraught to see her suffering and eventually dying in July 1960.

It was a difficult time for him emotionally and spiritually. In *A Grief Observed*,[10] written in 1961, he wrote out of his sense of loss and even gave free expression to his doubts about God and why God would allow such things to happen.

---

10. C. S. Lewis, *A Grief Observed,* 1st edition (London: Faber & Faber) 1961.

In 1985 a book was published called *Shadowlands*[11] which was subsequently made into a film. The book's sub-title is *The Story of C. S. Lewis and Joy Davidman* (which was her name before she married), and it tells the story of the unexpected relationship between the two. Jack's faith was sorely tested, but eventually that faith held firm.

Jack himself died on 22nd November 1963 (the same day as President Kennedy was assassinated in Dallas, Texas), and he is probably more famous now than he was in his lifetime. This would have surprised and maybe even embarrassed him, for he was a private sort of person. And yet he would surely be delighted that his influence has helped many others to come to faith and to live by faith, trusting in the promise of life abundant and life eternal.

It is fitting that on the last page of *Shadowlands*, there is an excerpt from the last of the seven Narnia stories, *The Last Battle*. It makes a suitable comment on the faith of C. S. Lewis, his trust in the theme of the famous gospel verse, John 3:16: 'God so loved the world that he gave his only Son that whoever believes in him should not perish but have eternal life'.

> '… the things that began to happen after that were so great and beautiful that I cannot write them. And for us this is the end of all the stories, and we can most truly say that they all lived happily ever after. But for them it was only the beginning of the real story. All their life in this world and all their adventures in Narnia had only been the cover and title-page: now at last they were beginning Chapter One of the Great Story which no one on earth has read: which goes on for ever; in which every chapter is better than the one before'.[12]

---

11. Brian Sibley, *Shadowlands,* 1st edition (London: Hodder and Stoughton, 1985).

12. C. S. Lewis, *The Complete Chronicles of Narnia* (Collins edition, London, 1998), 524.

Talking Points

1. Why do you think C. S. Lewis called himself a 'reluctant' convert?

2. Consider what C. S. Lewis would make of 2 Peter 1:16.

3. Could you answer anyone who said that 'in order to be a Christian you have to leave your brains outside the room'?

A Prayer

We are thankful for good stories and especially those that point us to the greatest story of all, your love for the world in sending Jesus so that whoever believes in Him should not perish but have everlasting life. Thank you for C. S. Lewis' many books on many subjects; help us, like him, to love you with all of our mind as well as heart, soul and strength.

Running the Race
Eric Liddell: An Athlete Who Wouldn't Compromise

For many people sport is important. They may not go so far as the famous football manager who said, 'Some people think football is a matter of life and death. I assure you, it's much more serious than that' – but they regard sport as very important.[1]

This chapter is about the life of a rugby player and athlete who achieved enormous success and fame in sport, but for whom sport was not the be-all and end-all of life. One day in 1924 an article in the *Scotsman* newspaper said of him, 'He is running another race and he will stay it even to the end'.[2]

The athlete's name was Eric Liddell and that comment was made a week after Eric had won the gold medal in the 400 metres race at the Olympic Games in Paris; the 'other race' was his life of Christian service.

It's a metaphor that is found in the Bible. Hebrews 12:1-2 talks about 'run[ning] with endurance the race that is set before us, looking to Jesus, the founder and perfecter of our faith', and it was probably on Paul's mind also when he wrote, 'Forgetting what

---

1. www.brainyquote.com/quotes/bill_shankly_312046 (accessed 28.6.18).

2. W. Steven, *Heroes of the Faith* (Church of Scotland Youth Committee, 1952), 86.

lies behind and straining forward to what lies ahead, I press on towards the goal for the prize of the upward call of God in Christ Jesus' (Philippians 3:13-14).

As a young man, Eric had achieved much in sport. He was a Scottish rugby internationalist and in track sport he was the holder of the 100 yards and 220 yards Scottish championships and of the 100, 220 and 440 yards British championships. He was the holder of the British record for the 100 yards sprint, so his selection to run for Britain in the 1924 Olympic Games in Paris was more or less a foregone conclusion.

Eric was keen to compete but some time before the Games he learned that the preliminary heats for the 100 metres were to be run on a Sunday. As a committed Christian who believed in keeping Sunday special, he announced that he was withdrawing from the event, which of course meant giving up the chance of Olympic glory (he didn't know what would happen after he made that decision).

There was much opposition to his decision and many people tried to persuade him to run; the British Amateur Athletic Association even tried to get the dates altered. Some people accused him of being unpatriotic – letting his country down.

But Eric believed that if he were to compete on a Sunday he would be letting his Lord down and that was something he wouldn't do. As his school headmaster had said of him years earlier, 'There was no pride or fuss about him but he knew what he stood for.'[3]

The fourth commandment says, 'Remember the Sabbath day, to keep it holy' (Exodus 20:8) and the New Testament encourages us to honour what it calls the Lord's Day, Sunday, the day of Jesus' resurrection from the dead. God wants us to observe Sunday as a day that is different from other days – a day of worship and fellowship and a day of rest.

---

3. www.ericliddell.org/about-us/eric-liddell/quotations/ (accessed 28.6.18).

If anyone had asked Eric later on (maybe they did) whether it had all been worth it, he would have said that faithfulness is the only proper response to 'the Son of God, who loved me and gave himself for me' (Galatians 2:20).

As it happens, Eric did go on to win Olympic success but his big decision was made before he knew that there would be any happy ending. He entered for the 400 metres event and it is said that just before one of the heats an unknown man came up and slipped into his hand a piece of paper on which were written the words of 1 Samuel 2:30: '"Those who honour me I will honour", says the Lord.' It seemed like a most fitting fulfilment of that word when Eric won the 400 metres event.

When asked for the secret of his success, he explained that he ran the first 200 metres as fast as he could and then for the second 200 metres, with God's help, he ran faster!

His story encourages us to be faithful to the God who loves us. Nowadays Sunday is treated by most people as an ordinary day or a fun day, and people who put God first by honouring His day may be regarded as old-fashioned or odd. But Eric Liddell's example encourages us to stand firm. God will honour those who honour Him. That does not necessarily mean immediate success (much less a gold medal!) but in the long run no-one will be the loser for putting God first on Sunday and every other day.

After the Olympic Games, Eric Liddell received great honour. His return from Paris was greeted by the kind of scenes associated nowadays with appearances by pop stars and 'celebrities' (there was no television coverage then – because there was no television! – B.B.C. radio was only two years old).

A week later, he graduated from Edinburgh University (Bachelor of Science) – and there were unprecedented scenes during and after the ceremony. Others were capped in the usual way but when Eric came to the platform, the Principal of the

University stopped him and said, 'Mr Liddell, you have shown that none could pass you except the examiners'! Afterwards he was borne through the streets by his (as they'd be called nowadays) fans.

One can only wonder whether such plaudits would be afforded today to someone who made the stand that Eric made. The 1981 film, *Chariots of Fire*,[4] was remarkably successful, winning four Academy Awards and being ranked nineteenth in the British Film Institute's list of the top 100 British films, but only a minority of people today would admire Eric's stand, much less emulate his decision.

One who has done so is the owner of The Entertainer chain of toyshops. In December 2017, news broadcasts were reporting on the fact that his 149 shops would not be opening on Christmas Eve, one of the big shopping days of the year, because that year 24th December was a Sunday. The owner is a Christian and he decided to stick with the normal pattern of opening six days a week but closing on Sunday, even if it might cost the firm a considerable loss of trade (some estimated about £2 million worth). It might be Christmas Eve, but it was Sunday and that was more important.

In Eric Liddell's case, there is an interesting comment in one of the biographies of his life. His wife Florence is quoted as saying, 'Eric always said that the great thing for him was that when he stood by his principles and refused to run in the 100 metres, he found that the 400 metres was really his race. He said he would never have known that otherwise. He would never have dreamed of trying the 400 at the Olympics.'[5] No, no-one will lose out in the long run for being faithful to the Lord.

---

4. Hugh Hudson, *Chariots of Fire*, written by Colin Welland, produced by David Puttnam, starring Ian Charleson as Eric Liddell (United Kingdom:20th Century Fox, 1981).

5. Recorded in Sally Magnusson's *The Flying Scotsman*, (Quartet, 1981), 45.

After his graduation, Eric was honoured at a dinner in Edinburgh, at which a Court of Session Judge paid tribute to one who, he said, would not shield himself behind such easy phrases as, 'When in Rome, do as the Romans do.'

And the following day (as stated earlier) the *Scotsman* reported on Eric's reply: 'The modesty and simplicity and directness of his words went straight to the heart. No adulation, no fame, no flattery can ever affect this youth with the clean-cut features, the level eyes and the soft voice. He made us quickly realise that running was not to be his career. He was training to be a missionary in China ... He is running another race, and he will stay it even to the end.'[6]

After graduation he embarked on missionary training and then undertook a year of evangelistic meetings and campaigns (one of the many venues in which he spoke was the school I attended; I wish I had been there that day) before departing for China.

In the introduction we referred to the question often asked in adolescent years, 'Does it work?' Does faith in Christ actually make any difference to anything?

An interesting response to that question was given by a swimming pool attendant who told a friend that Eric's messages at the local Y.M.C.A. had even made a difference in the pool! I don't think he meant people were swimming faster or further; the mission had made a difference to people's attitudes and behaviour. True commitment to Christ will show one way or another; as the Bible says, it bears fruit (John 15:4; Galatians 5:22-23; James 2:17).

In July 1925 Eric set off for China. He was driven to the railway station in a decorated carriage, pulled by some fellow-students. It's hard for us today to imagine the scene at Edinburgh's Waverley Station as crowds gathered to see him off and he was asked to say

---

6. W. Steven, *Heroes of the Faith* (Church of Scotland Youth Committee, 1952), 86.

a few words to them. Instead he led the crowd in the impromptu singing of a hymn! It was Isaac Watts' paraphrase of Psalm 72:

> Jesus shall reign where'er the sun
> Does his successive journeys run;
> His kingdom stretch from shore to shore
> Till moons shall wax and wane no more.[7]

It was the start of a journey that led to his service as a missionary for the next twenty years. He joined the staff of the Anglo-Chinese College in Tientsin (where he had been born to his missionary parents) as a science and sports teacher. It was a decision which has been described as one that seemed perfectly logical to him and perfectly illogical to those who didn't understand his faith. He had famously said that God made him fast – he also said that God made him for China, and to China he went.

He worked in Tientsin until 1938 when he undertook evangelistic work based in Siaochang. It was in China that he met and then married a Canadian lady called Florence. They had three daughters but Eric never saw the third. Florence was pregnant when war broke out and, with the Imperial Japanese Army advancing through China, Eric insisted that she and the girls should leave for Canada.

He himself refused to leave China and in January 1942 he was arrested by the Japanese and interned at Weihsien – in a former American Presbyterian Mission compound which the Japanese then called a Civilian Assembly Centre but which really a prison camp. Chinese bandits and Japanese soldiers had vandalised the place; there was no heating, little light and the toilets wouldn't flush so that the stench was awful. There was a grey eight foot high wall and watchtowers from which searchlights shone down while

---

7. Hymn, 'Jesus shall reign', by Isaac Watts, 1674-1748.

guards stood with machine guns and/or swords and sometimes Alsatian dogs.

The camp was about the size of two football pitches, with about 1,800 people crammed into a space measuring roughly 200 x 150 yards. Prisoners were allowed a shower once a week in communal blocks that offered little privacy, and the whole place was infested with rats, flies, maggots, mosquitoes, scorpions and other bugs.

In these dreadful conditions, Eric devoted himself to the welfare of his fellow-prisoners; some called him 'Uncle Eric'. At one point he even refused an opportunity to return to Great Britain when the prime minister, Winston Churchill, brokered a deal; instead Eric arranged for a pregnant woman from the camp to take his place.

He was renowned for the practical care he extended to other people; for instance, back in Siaochang there had been a dust storm that caused sand and grit to creep under doors and windows to cover everything; Eric rose before 4.30 am to clean up the mess with pan, broom and duster, working as quietly as possible so that no-one's sleep was disturbed.

A group of children and teenagers arrived in camp once from a missionary school (Chefoo) and one day when they were diverting themselves by having a race, Eric got involved. The kids saw an older bald man rather than an Olympic gold medallist and they were amazed when he managed to keep up with them! One of them was a fifteen-year-old named Steve who later recalled, 'He was my role model. He was also everyone's hero'.

Is that exaggerated admiration? One of his biographers researched and travelled extensively and his conclusions about Eric's character are worth recording:

> 'Sceptical questions are always going to be asked when someone is portrayed without apparent faults. Liddell can sound too virtuous and too honourable to be true, as if those who knew him

were either misremembering or consciously mythologizing. Not so. The evidence is too overwhelming to be dismissed as easily as that. Amid the myriad moral dilemmas in Weihsien, Liddell's forbearance was remarkable. No one could recall a solitary act of envy, pettiness, hubris or self-aggrandizement from him. He bad-mouthed nobody. He didn't bicker. He lived daily by the most unselfish credo, which was to help others practically and emotionally.'[8]

The same author wrote, 'His story has no full stop'.[9] That could be said about his enduring legacy and example in this world, as his story is remembered through books and films. It can also be said in relation to the faith he held dear as a man in Christ who believed in the reality of God's promise of eternal life to His believing people.

Eventually Eric became ill as the result of a brain tumour and he died on 21st February 1945, aged forty-three.

In Britain he is sometimes known as 'The Flying Scotsman', but he was born in China and there he is remembered as the country's first Olympic champion. There is a museum there which features his story and in August 2015 a statue of him was unveiled – a remarkable honour for a Christian missionary in a communist country.

He believed the gospel is true, that it works and that commitment to Christ is indeed 'worth it'. His example says to us: 'Let us run with endurance the race that is set before us, looking to Jesus, the founder and perfecter of our faith, who for the joy that was set before him endured the cross, despising the shame, and is seated at the right hand of the throne of God.' (Hebrews 12:1-2)

---

8. Duncan Hamilton, *For The Glory* (London: Penguin, 2017), 10.

9. Ibid.

Talking Points

1. How would you answer the allegation that Eric Liddell was unpatriotic in refusing to run for his country that Sunday in Paris?

2. What do we learn from the image of running as used in Hebrews 12:1-2 and Philippians 3:13-14?

3. Consider the statement, 'In the long run no-one will be the loser for putting God first on Sunday and every other day.' How special is Sunday to you, and are there things you believe you should/shouldn't do on Sunday?

A Prayer

For the health and strength you have given us we thank you, Lord, and for the enjoyment of sport and fitness. Help us look after the lives you have given us in every way and to honour you as Lord and Master on Sunday and every other day. Strengthen us to lay aside everything that keeps us back and to run the Christian race with endurance, looking to Jesus all our days.

'Whoever Loses His Life …'
Jim Elliot: Pioneer Missionary and Martyr

Our question, 'Is it worth it?', is one that many would ask about the subject of this chapter. Jim Elliot was only twenty-eight years old when he was brutally murdered by the banks of a river in Ecuador, along with four other missionaries. Many people would simply say, 'What a waste! Why did he put himself in that position? And why did God let it happen?'

Yet one of the most widely-quoted Christian sayings comes from young Jim Elliot. He was thinking of the charge that it's foolish to risk your life for Christ's sake and he wrote in his journal, 'He is no fool who gives what he cannot keep to gain what he cannot lose.' The 'gain' he mentioned is the gift of God's salvation which includes the promise of eternal glory with Him and Jim no doubt had Jesus' words in mind: 'What does it profit a man to gain the whole world and forfeit his soul?' In the previous verse Jesus said, 'Whoever would save his life will lose it, but whoever loses his life for my sake and the gospel's will save it' (Mark 8:35-36).

Jim literally lost his life for the sake of Christ and His gospel but, whether that is the cost or not, Jesus' call is the call for a radical commitment that puts His will first. Jim Elliot took that seriously; not for him the idea of Christianity as a leisurely stroll or a 'nice' religion for children and old ladies! Of course, the gospel is for children and for old ladies, but Jim's commitment was rugged, realistic and ready to take risks for Christ's sake.

On 2nd January 1956 Jim and the four others – Ed McCully, Nate Saint, Roger Youderian and Pete Fleming – took the short flight over the jungle to land on the banks of the Curaray River in eastern Ecuador. It was the culmination of a long time of patient preparation and they were going to bring the good news of Jesus to the tribe, the Aucas (now known as Huaorani or Waorani). A short time later, however, the bodies of all five lay on the riverbank, speared to death.

I was ten years old at the time and I remember the shock it caused as news travelled (even in pre-internet days) round the world. It seemed so awful. They were young men with the best of motives, and many wondered why such a dreadful thing should happen. Was it a waste?

Jim had grown up in a Christian family in the American city of Portland, Oregon. He heard visiting missionaries and came to feel that when Jesus said His people should go and spread the gospel He meant that they should go and spread the gospel! Why should people still live and die without any knowledge of what Hebrews 2:3 calls 'such a great salvation'?

It was later at a missionary training course at Oklahoma University that a former missionary to the Quichuas of Ecuador told Jim about the Aucas and Jim was immediately excited at the thought of seeking to reach a tribe as yet untouched by civilisation and who knew nothing of Christ and His gospel ('Auca' is the Quichua word for savages).

In February 1952 he and Pete Fleming sailed to Quito in Ecuador where they set about learning Spanish. After a year they moved to a small Quichua village where they witnessed for Christ, and many Quichuas became Christians.

Jim learned more about the Auca Indians and believed God wanted him to tell them the good news. But how? The Aucas were cut off from the world at large and they had consistently killed outsiders who ventured into their area. They had forced the closure of an oil drilling site nearby (petrol is the country's main export) as people were afraid to work there.

Ed McCully told Jim about an Auca girl called Dayuma who, as a teenager, had fled the tribe after a vicious family feud, and she made it clear that the Aucas couldn't be trusted – they might appear friendly but then turn round and kill you.

How could Jim and the others involved in what was known as Operation Auca let this tribe know that they had no hostile intentions and wanted to befriend them?

We can learn about it from Jim himself – in the last letter he wrote to his parents. It was written on 28th December 1955 and he refers to Nate Saint, who was a pilot with MAF (Mission Aviation Fellowship), and the inventive method he devised to initiate contact with the Aucas. He discovered that if he lowered a bucket on a rope from his plane and then flew in tight circles, the bucket remained almost stationary.

In his letter Jim refers to this method of trying to let the Aucas know that they wanted to be their friends. They would put useful things like a kettle or machete in the bucket and lower it. After several such drops, the Aucas responded by sending up gifts in return, such as a woven headband, peanuts and two parrots (live).

After three months of such contact, the team felt it was time to make ground contact, and this is what Jim wrote on 28th December to his mum and dad:

'By the time this reaches you, Ed and Pete and I and another fellow will have attempted with Nate a contact with the Aucas. We have prayed for this and prepared for several months. Some time ago on survey flights Nate located two groups of their houses and ever since that time we have made weekly friendship flights, dropping gifts and shouting phrases from a loudspeaker in their language. Nate has used his drop-cord system to land things right at their doorstep and we have received several gifts back from them.

'Our plan is to go downriver and land on a beach we have surveyed not far from their place, build a tree house which I have prefabricated with our power-saw here, then invite them over by calling to them from the plane. … I don't have to remind you that these are completely naked savages who have never had any contact with white men other than killing. They do not have firearms, but kill with long chonta-wood lances. They have no word for God in their language, only for devils and spirits, I know you will pray. Our orders are 'the gospel to every creature'. Your loving son and brother, Jim.'[1]

On Friday 6th January three Aucas suddenly appeared out of the jungle – one man and two women (one called Gimade who was Dayuma's sister). They had walked the four miles to the riverbank and the missionaries greeted them. They made friendly contact; Nate even took the man up in the plane and showed him his own village from the air. Later the three Aucas left with gifts given to them.

There was no sign of them on the Saturday and then on the Sunday Nate took off to circle the Auca village and see what was happening. From the air he saw a number of Aucas making their way along the beach, so when he landed he announced to the others, 'This is it, guys! They're on their way!'

They had lunch and sang together the hymn, 'We rest on Thee', which has the last verse:

---

1. Elisabeth Elliot, *Shadow of the Almighty* (London: Hodder & Stoughton, 1958).

> We rest on Thee, our Shield and our Defender,
> Thine is the battle, Thine shall be the praise
> When passing through the gates of pearly splendour,
> Victors, we rest with Thee through endless days.[2]

Jim had once written in his journal, 'I seek not a long life but a full one, like you, Lord Jesus', and Jim's widow Elisabeth wrote: 'Before four-thirty that afternoon the quiet waters of the Curaray flowed over the bodies of the five comrades, slain by the men they had come to win for Christ. The world called it a nightmare of tragedy. The world did not recognise the truth of the second clause in Jim Elliot's credo: "He is no fool who gives what he cannot keep to gain what he cannot lose."'[3]

Everything had looked hopeful – but for some reason the Aucas had turned hostile. They hurled their sharp spears at the five missionaries, killing all of them.

Elisabeth waited to hear news on the two-way radio, only to be met with silence. She and the other wives knew something was very seriously wrong and the next morning another missionary pilot flew over the beach and saw only the damaged plane. After news had spread round the world, an American team went to Ecuador and found the bodies of the five men.

Was it 'worth it'? It didn't seem so. Certainly if this world is all there is, it would have to be counted a waste. That's what the apostle Paul wrote in 1 Corinthians 15:19 – 'If in Christ we have hope in this life only, we are of all people most to be pitied.' Why? It would be pitiable because Jim's death at twenty-eight years old would be his total loss of everything for ever. But what did Jesus say? He was speaking about His own coming death (aged about thirty-three) and He likened it to a seed falling

---

2. Hymn, 'We Rest on Thee', by Edith Gilling Cherry, 1872-97.

3. From *Shadow of the Almighty*, (London: Hodder & Stoughton, 1958).

into the earth and being buried, but then bearing much fruit. If we didn't know about that process, it would seem completely miraculous to us, whether we think of fields of corn or potatoes in our own garden.

A similar thing could be said about Jim Elliot's death. So far as he himself is concerned – Jesus went on, 'Whoever loves his life loses it, and whoever hates his life in this world will keep it for eternal life' (John 12:24-25). My Study Bible comments (you might almost think the writer had Jim Elliot in mind), 'Hates his life in this world means "thinks so little of his life, and so much of God, that he is willing to sacrifice it all for God".'[4]

So when we ask the question, 'Is it worth it?' we need to remember that this world is not the only world and this life is not the only life. The gospel tells us that Jim's twenty-eight years in this world are the merest fraction of the 'eternal life' that is God's gift for His people.

And what's more, Jim's death has in fact borne a great deal of fruit. He had longed for more people to become missionaries and his story has been the inspiration of many more than he could ever have imagined. Within weeks another pilot continued the flights over the Auca settlement and more than twenty others from the United States applied to take Nate Saint's place. It is said also that more than a thousand college students volunteered for missionary service as a direct response to the story of Operation Auca – and what happened afterwards.

Shortly after Jim's death, his widow Elisabeth wrote, 'The prayers of the widows themselves are for the Aucas. We look forward to the day when these savages will join us in Christian praise.'[5] This is an astonishing statement which is baffling by the standards of this world; what kind of inner transformation does

---

4. ESV Student Study Bible (Collins, 2011), 1418.

5. Elisabeth Elliot, *Through Gates Of Splendour* (London: Hodder & Stoughton, 1957), 189.

the Spirit of Jesus Christ make in people's lives to produce such a prayer and such a desire!

Elisabeth had also come to Ecuador as a missionary to the Quichua people. For the first year she and Jim worked in different regions until they were married in 1953 and served together.

After Jim was killed, Elisabeth wouldn't give up on the people and she continued to live in the region with their daughter Valerie and also Rachel Saint, the sister of one of the other martyrs. She developed contact with the Aucas and eventually learned that the tribe had thought that the foreigners were coming to enslave them and spoil their lives – that's why they killed them.

Elisabeth told them the gospel and Dayuma became the first Auca convert, before many others became Christians, including some of those involved in killing the five men.

Dayuma also helped the missionaries to learn the Waorani language which is virtually unrelated to any other language and which had never been studied previously, and became an influential person in the tribe. She travelled and spoke at meetings in the United States and died on 1st March 2014. Elisabeth herself worked in Ecuador until December 1961 when she and Valerie moved to America where she worked as an author and speaker, sharing her experiences. She died in 2015 at the age of eighty-eight.

The Bible says, 'If anyone is in Christ, he is a new creation' (2 Corinthians 5:17); if anyone doubts it – doubts that Christianity is true, works and is worth it – he might well consider this story which (wouldn't you say?) is inexplicable apart from the life-changing power of Christ.

TALKING POINTS

1. What do you think Jim Elliot would say to anyone who suggested that he had just wasted his life? What did he mean when he wrote his now famous words, 'He is no fool who gives what he cannot keep to gain what he cannot lose'?

2. Consider how John 12:24 is seen in the life of Jim Elliot (and his four friends).

3. Do you and your church know of any missionaries today whom you could support with your interest, messages and prayer?

A PRAYER

Thank you, Father, for all who have left home and family to spread the gospel, especially those who face threats and danger for the sake of Christ. Help me to know your will for my life and where you want me to serve you, and help us and our church to take an active interest in some missionaries for whom we can pray. Thank you for the life and testimony of Jim Elliot.

'PTL' (Praise the Lord)
Joni Eareckson Tada: Paralyzed but Undaunted

We begin this chapter with some words that are addressed to people who experience suffering of one kind or another. This world contains many hurting people, old and young, and indeed the very existence of so much suffering and pain has led some people to question whether Christianity can be true, whether it really works and whether it's worth bothering about.

The words that follow are words of encouragement and hope, especially for people of any age who feel that life isn't fair or they have been cheated in some way.

> 'When life seems wild, crazy and utterly out of control. It is not. When it seems as though God has forgotten you or turned His back on you to tinker with some other universe, He has not. When it seems like you have somehow fallen out of His favour, been edged outside the circle of His protection, or missed the bus on His love, you have not.'[1]

From many people, words like these might seem hollow and even cruel, but they are the words of someone who knows what she is talking about and who is, if we can put it this way, qualified

---

1. Joni Eareckson Tada, *A Lifetime of Wisdom* (Minnesota: Zondervan, 2009), 180.

to speak. They were written by Joni (pronounced like Johnny) Eareckson Tada who has been in a wheelchair for fifty years since a terrible accident left her without any feeling below her shoulders.

It was a hot summer day in 1967. Joni was seventeen, a bright teenager from a happy family, a girl who loved horse-riding, lacrosse, hockey – and swimming. This day she and some friends were at Chesapeake Bay in Maryland, U.S.A. She took a breath, dived into the lake and then – in her own words:

> 'Many things happened simultaneously. I felt my head strike something hard and unyielding. At the same time, clumsily and crazily, my body sprawled out of control. I heard or felt a loud electric buzzing, an unexplainable inner sensation. It was something like an electric shock … I heard the underwater sound of crunching, grinding sand. I was lying face down on the bottom.'[2]

Her sister Kathy managed to get hold of her, but Joni realised that she couldn't feel anything in her limbs or lower body.

Someone called 911 and soon the sound of an ambulance siren was heard. Joni was rushed to hospital where she heard a doctor saying it looked like a fracture-dislocation at the fourth and fifth cervical level (broken neck to you and me).

Then she saw someone holding a pair of electric hair clippers. 'Please, not my hair!' she said, but her hair was removed as she was prepared for surgery. For several days she drifted in and out of consciousness, lying in a frame that could be flipped over every so often.

Days and weeks went by after that and it began to dawn on Joni that she wasn't about to recover and be discharged from hospital. Dark despair and depression filled her mind and heart

---

2. Most of the quotations in this chapter have come from the books, '*Joni*' and '*A Lifetime of Wisdom*'). Joni Eareckson, *Joni* (London: Pickering & Inglis, 1976) and Joni Eareckson Tada, *A Lifetime of Wisdom* (Minnesota: Zondervan, 2009).

as she felt that although she was still a teenager there was nothing to look forward to except a lifetime of sitting in a wheelchair. Sometimes she even pleaded with others to help her end her life by giving her an overdose of pills or cutting her wrist.

After three and a half months she was moved to a rehabilitation centre and she began to hope again – this was, she dreamed, where she would learn to walk and begin her life again. But it wasn't to be.

Her first book (she has now written more than fifty, and her *Joni* has been translated into forty-five languages with a circulation of four million) was subtitled, 'The unforgettable story of a young woman's struggle against quadriplegia and depression'. She was seventeen; life should be opening out before her.

She had had a Christian upbringing in a loving family and she had committed her life to Christ, but in dark moments she would now sometimes think, 'Who, or What, is God? Certainly not a personal Being who cares for individuals. What's the use of believing when your prayers fall on deaf ears?'

She wasn't interested in trite answers; many years later she would write, 'When your heart is being wrung out like a sponge, an orderly list of 'sixteen good biblical reasons as to why this is happening' can sting like salt in a wound'.[3] This is why I suggested that the words at the start of this chapter might sound hollow from some people, but Joni hasn't just had a bad dose of flu or mourned the loss of a family pet. She has been through so much – so much that destroys faith for some people – but she has come through with a faith that is strong, vibrant and infectious.

She has discovered the reality of a faith that centres in One who, as the Bible says, is able to sympathise with our weaknesses, One who has suffered and is able to help (Hebrews 2:18 and 4:15).

---

3. http://www.joniandfriends.org/radio/4-minute/answers/ (accessed 28.6.18).

Joni would encourage us to continue trusting Him, the One who has given her strength for these many years since that disastrous accident changed her life altogether.

Among her other talents, she is a fine singer and in one of her albums she sings a song which she wrote herself. It is called 'When Pretty Things Get Broken' and the following are the first two verses with chorus:

> I have a piece of china, a lovely porcelain vase;
> It holds such lovely flowers, captures everybody's gaze.
> But fragile things do slip and fall as everybody knows
> And when my vase came crushing down those tears began
> to flow.
>
> My life was just like china, a lovely thing to me,
> Full of porcelain promises of all that I might be.
> But fragile things do slip and fall as everybody knows
> And when my life came crashing down those tears began
> to flow.
>
> But don't we all cry when pretty things get broken?
> Don't we all sigh at such an awful loss?
> Jesus will dry those tears as He has spoken
> 'Cause He was the One broken on the cross.[4]

During her time in rehabilitation, Joni sometimes believed that she would get better – even that God would heal her miraculously – but she came to accept her situation and learned to do what Scripture says – to give thanks in everything (1 Thessalonians 5:18); she once wrote about developing the habit of giving thanks (something we could all learn from her).

---

4. www.joniandfriends.org/radio/4-minute/when-pretty-things-get-broken/ (accessed 5.6.18).

She was encouraged to develop her artistic talents, holding a pen or brush between her teeth, and her drawings are astonishingly inspiring. She usually puts 'PTL' on her paintings – short for 'Praise the Lord', and her artwork has become famous.

When Joni was twenty, one of her sisters introduced her to a friend called Steve who was only sixteen but who became a great helper and encourager. She felt at ease with Steve who encouraged her to believe that Christianity is true and that it 'works'. He said that in the church to which he belonged they had seen many remarkable transformations through God's power: a couple on the verge of divorce had been brought together again, someone heavily into dope had been saved, a girl who was messed up inside had been straightened out by the Lord.

In many conversations Steve was able to explain Bible truth to her in such a way that it was as if the Lord was speaking directly to her, and, through many ups and downs, Joni grew in faith. She came to see that she had previously accepted Christianity pretty much without question; she examined other philosophical and theological points of view but felt that God was providing answers to her questions.

Despite everything that had happened to her, she grew spiritually and came to trust God's sovereignty over everything and His ability to work 'in everything' for the good of those who love Him (Romans 8:28).

As she developed her artistic ability, she would also give her testimony to various groups, encouraging others (including us) as she would say, 'God's Word is true. I know it's true because I've experienced it. I've found it to be so.'[5]

---

5. https://christianlibrary.org.au/index.php?option=com_content&view=article&id=87:oni-a-others-quotes-on-suffering&catid=40:school-of-suffering&Itemid=72 (accessed 28.6.18).

Joni had friendships with several people, including young men, and eventually in 1982 she married Ken Tada, a school teacher who has supported and loved her over the years. This included support through the diagnosis of breast cancer in 2010, which she survived after surgery and chemotherapy.

Besides being an artist and a singer, Joni has also acted – she actually played the part of herself in the film of her early life. She has described the experience as one of her favourite memories (and by the way the film *Chariots of Fire* is her favourite movie – mentioned in our chapter 10).

In 1979 she established 'Joni And Friends' as an organisation that helps families affected by disability and she is now an international advocate for people with disabilities. She serves as Chief Executive Officer of the Joni And Friends International Disability Center which opened its doors in 1997.

There is also a daily radio programme that reaches over a million listeners a week, they run family retreats for special needs families from all across the United States and another amazing project is 'Wheels for the World'. This ministry has provided over 100,000 wheelchairs, along with Bibles, to needy disabled individuals in developing nations – they refurbish wheelchairs and other mobility devices through volunteers in prisons and then ship them overseas where physiotherapists give them to people in developing nations.

Joni's life has turned out very differently from what she would have expected as a young girl. Earlier on she was so depressed that she desperately wanted to commit suicide – a far cry from the full life she has lived during the last fifty years in her wheelchair. Far from wanting to end her life she actively opposes the current pressure towards the acceptance of assisted suicide.

One of her most moving drawings is the drawing of an empty wheelchair with a 'For Sale' ticket tied to it – no longer needed.

Such is the gospel hope for all who receive Christ and His complete salvation. She looks forward to God's gift of a brand new and glorified body, to being able to stand and stretch and do aerobics and comb her own hair and blow her own nose – even to be able to wipe away her own tears, except that there won't be any tears then (Revelation 21:4).

She doesn't claim to know all the answers to all the questions that can be asked about suffering and why God allows certain things to happen.

But she demonstrates a better 'answer' than an intellectual one – the practical life of faith and trust in a God who has won our salvation through the epitome of undeserved suffering and who says to us, '… I am with you always …' (Matthew 28:20), 'even though you walk through the valley of the shadow of death, you need fear no evil' (Psalm 23:4) and 'As your days, so shall your strength be' (Deuteronomy 33:25).

She has referred to the apostle Paul's words about trials in 2 Timothy 1:12 – not 'I know *why* this is happening to me' but 'I know *whom* I have believed.'

The other people described in this book had never heard of the internet, but Joni has (although she hadn't back in 1967 when she broke her neck) and the website of Joni And Friends is well worth visiting: www.joniandfriends.org.

On the website there's a section headed, 'People that inspire Joni'. She writes there: 'In our journey through life, we all need people to inspire us along the way—and I'm no exception. I thank God for sending me true models of inspiration, and I have the pleasure of introducing you to some of them here.'

There can be little doubt that for many other people Joni herself is just such a person.

TALKING POINTS

1. 'The existence of so much suffering and pain has led some people to question whether Christianity can be true, whether it really works and whether it's worth bothering about.' What do you think?

2. Why do you think Romans 8:28 has been such an important verse for Joni?

3. How can Hebrews 4:15 help when we are faced with troubles in life?

A PRAYER

We give thanks, Lord, for the way in which Joni's life has been and remains an inspiration to so many people, especially people with disabilities. Bless her continuing ministry and help us, whatever trials we may meet, to trust in you as the Lord who has the whole world in your hands and who works in everything for good with those who love you.

Epilogue

This book has recorded some heroic stories which I hope have been inspiring as well as interesting.

However, Christianity is not about hero worship. There's far more to it than that and Jesus Himself is so much more than a hero. The Bible presents Him to us as Lord and Saviour. It says He is the way, the truth and the life (John 14:6), and Acts 4:12 spells out the challenge to faith very clearly: 'There is salvation in no one else, for there is no other name under heaven given among men by which we must be saved.'

It was Peter and John who spoke these words in front of the enemies of Jesus (in the Jewish council), and we are told that when these enemies saw the boldness of Peter and John and remembered that they were ordinary men (not superstars, intellectuals or celebrities), they couldn't deny that there was something special about them – they had been with Jesus. Nor could they deny the fact (because it was a fact) that the once-lame man whom Peter and John had cured by the power of Jesus was walking around Jerusalem. All they could do was feebly admonish Peter and John and instruct them to stop telling people about Jesus. As if …!

Well, no one could deny that there was also something special about the twelve people featured in this book. They represent different periods of history, different nationalities and different occupations; they had different backgrounds, personalities and areas of work. They would probably all claim to be 'ordinary' (as if anyone is ordinary), they certainly wouldn't claim to be perfect, and for whatever they achieved they would want to deflect all praise and glory to Jesus.

At the same time, it is also true that they do give inspiration and encouragement for Christian discipleship.

- One characteristic of some (if not all) of them is courage. These people weren't weaklings who just followed Christ so long as everything went well for them; nor were they wimps who would just 'do what everybody else is doing'. They didn't follow the crowd; they stood by what they believed, whatever the cost.

  Most of them lived in times when they didn't have the home comforts which we enjoy. For many of them, life was hard, but – to paraphrase John Bunyan's hymn quoted earlier – if you want to see true valour, look at the kind of people described in this book. No discouragement made them give up their commitment to labour night and day to be servants of the King.

- Many had to overcome obstacles in life – blindness, paralysis, imprisonment. As Hebrews 11:27 intriguingly says of Moses, they too 'endured as seeing him who is invisible.' They found that God's amazing grace was sufficient to bring them through many dangers, toils and snares. Their attitude was that expressed in the hymn:

My times are in Thy hand, whatever they may be,
Pleasing or painful, dark or bright, as best may seem to Thee.
My times are in Thy hand; why should I doubt or fear?
My Father's hand will never cause His child a needless tear.[6]

- Patience is another thing. These men and women lived lives of discipleship and faithfulness. For example, we saw that it took Wilberforce more than twenty years to abolish the slave trade. It is often said about David Livingstone that he didn't produce many converts, but he laboured with patience and he certainly prepared the way for others who would come after him: 'May they not forget the pioneers who worked in the thick gloom with few rays to cheer except such as flow from faith in God's promises!' Livingstone's parents-in-law, Robert and Mary Moffat were pioneer missionaries in Botswana (then Bechuanaland) who at one point sent home for some communion silver, even though there weren't yet any converts or any Church; they laboured in faith and with patience.

  As is often said, God looks for faithfulness, not success. If success comes, that's great, but His call is for people who are ready to – what was it – deny self, take up your cross and follow Him (Mark 8:34).

- Reliance on God's Word is another characteristic of the people described in this book. What was written about Mary Slessor could have been said of them all:

  'The spiritual strengths in Mary Slessor's life can be traced to the fact that for her the Word of God was her

---

6. Hymn, "My Times are in Thy hand", by William Freeman Lloyd, 1791-1853.

daily food, her solemn and sufficient guide through life, and that which she could completely rely on.'[7]

As she herself said, 'The Bible has nurtured my entire life.'

It is no ordinary book. The first verse I ever memorised is Psalm 119:105 (NIV) – 'Your word is a lamp to my feet and a light on my path.' If you have been taught the things of God from early in life, it would be good to heed Paul's words to young Timothy in 2 Timothy 3:14-16: 'As for you, continue in what you have learned and have firmly believed, knowing from whom you learned it and how from childhood you have been acquainted with the sacred writings, which are able to make you wise for salvation through faith in Christ Jesus. All Scripture is breathed out by God and profitable for teaching, for reproof, for correction, and for training in righteousness.'

You may have noticed other characteristics of these twelve servants of God. None of them would claim great things for themselves but they are commended here as people more worthy of emulation than some of the 'celebrities' of today's culture who often point in a very different direction, with lifestyles very different from the way of wisdom found in Scripture.

The book of Psalms starts off with the up-front statement (quoting from the New Living Translation): 'Oh, the joys of those who do not follow the advice of the wicked, or stand around with sinners, or join in with mockers. But they delight in the law of the LORD, meditating on it day and night. They are like trees planted along the riverbank, bearing fruit each season.

---

7. Bruce McLennan, Mary Slessor: *A Life on the Altar for God* (Tain: Christian Focus, 2014), 168.

Their leaves never wither, and they prosper in all they do.'
(Psalm 1:1-3 NLT)

In the introduction we referred to the idea that in their
teenage years people assess and sometimes question much that
has been passed on to them by other people. This was mentioned
in a book written more than fifty years ago, but I am sure that
the assertion is still true:

'Like all other childish assumptions, religious beliefs are
likely to be subjected to the test of three questions – "Is it true?"
"Does it work?" "Is it worth it?"'[8]

We have raised these issues throughout this book, and it's
time to say: well, *is* it true? does *it* work? *is* it worth it? What do
you think?

It's not a question of whether Christianity is a 'nice' religion
or whether we would like it to be true. The gospel of Christ is
not some kind of feel-good story, much less a fairy tale, to be left
behind with Cinderella and Aladdin.

- Is it true? There is a God who made everything and
  who has revealed Himself in many ways and supremely
  in Jesus Christ – incarnate, crucified and risen – who
  says, 'Behold, I stand at the door and knock. If anyone
  hears my voice and opens the door, I will come in'
  (Revelation 3:20). He calls us to trust Him and to love
  Him with all our heart, soul, mind and strength.

- Does it work? If the first question is about the truthfulness
  of Christianity, this question is about its relevance.
  The stories told show that it does make a difference –
  whether it's protecting people from Nazi cruelty, going
  to a remote tribe to tell them the gospel, or coping with
  blindness, paralysis or unjust imprisonment. It certainly

---

8. Saward and Eastman, *Christian Youth Groups* (London: Scripture Union, 1965), 25.

does make a difference; it's the same power that enabled Paul to say in quick succession, 'I press on towards the goal', 'I have learned in whatever situation I am to be content' and 'I can do all things through him who strengthens me' (Philippians 3:14; 4:11; 4:13).

• And is it worth it? We quoted Jim Elliot's famous word from his journal: 'He is no fool who gives what he cannot keep to gain what he cannot lose.'

May God give us such a perspective, the kind that David Livingstone had when he spoke in many towns and universities during his first visit home after sixteen years in central Africa. He said, 'People talk of the sacrifice I have made in spending so much of my life in Africa. Away with the word in such a view, and with such a thought! It is emphatically no sacrifice. Say rather it is a privilege. I never made a sacrifice. Of this we ought not to talk, when we remember the great sacrifice which He made who left His Father's throne on high to give Himself for us.'[9]

It is true. It does work. It is worth it.

---

9. Speaking in Cambridge in December 1857, quoted in: W. G. Blaikie, *The Life of David Livingstone* (John Murray, 1903), 190.

It can be difficult to ask questions, far less answer them. Perhaps you've felt that sometimes the questions you really want to ask just can't be answered. They're too difficult; too embarrassing; and perhaps you shouldn't be asking them anyway. William Edgar takes a selection of twenty-four questions just like that – questions that are asked by young adults just like you – and gives a biblical, common sense, unpatronising answer to each. Edgar tackles issues such as 'Where is God?' 'Can we trust the Bible?' 'What about love and sex?' 'Does God love gay people?' 'When will the world end?' 'Are there vampires?' 'Can I have real friends?'

ISBN: 978-1-78191-143-3

• C. S. Lewis •
THE STORY TELLER

Derick Bingham

Adventures into another world, stories of mystery and wonder, these are what fascinated and excited Clive. He was just a boy but would sit for hours writing stories where animals came to life and lived and spoke just like human beings. This little boy grew up to become the world famous writer C. S. Lewis. However, throughout his life he preferred to be called Jack. The reasons for this peculiar change of name and other interesting facts and stories about C. S. Lewis are retold in this book. It was written in the centenary year of his birth – this is a reprint. This book takes you into the life of C. S. Lewis, the child, the scholar, the husband, the writer and the believer in God. Derick Bingham has researched this book thoroughly and has lovingly retold the story of this great storyteller.

ISBN: 978-1-85792-487-9

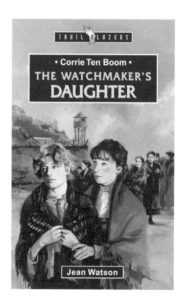

The story of Corrie ten Boom has inspired millions of people all over the world. Jean Watson is a skilful author and presents Corrie's stirring life and challenging hope-filled message for young readers.

The Watchmaker's Daughter traces the life of this outstanding Christian woman from her childhood in Haarlem, through her suffering in Nazi concentration camps, to her world-wide ministry to the handicapped and underprivileged.

This exciting victorious book will allow you to meet this beloved woman and learn of God's wonderful provision and blessing through adversity.

ISBN: 978-1-85792-116-8

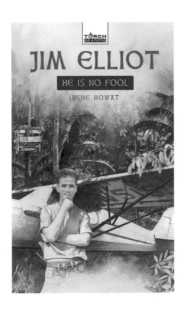

Jim Elliot had a loving wife, a beautiful little girl, and a reason for real joy. God had called him to bring the good news of Jesus Christ to the Auca Indians. The love of Christ not only thrilled him but also gave him peace. Jim would spend the rest of his life bringing Jesus to the lost Aucas ... but the rest of Jim's life was only a matter of months.

Jim had realised for quite some time what serving God really meant. This is the story of Jim's love for a fighting people and of his fight for a loving God. When his life ended, the work went on and many of the Auca Indians today have the same reason that Jim Elliot had for real joy.

ISBN: 978-1-84550-064-1

Joni Eareckson is a well-known Christian speaker and author from America but there was a day when she was a teenage girl in a bathing costume with nothing on her mind but boys, make up and her beloved horse, Tumbleweed.

However, all that changed one morning when an innocent dive turned into a tragic accident. Joni's story is a wonderful testimony to God's grace and power in someone's life.

Healing may have been an amazing miracle that didn't happen but Joni's ongoing work with thousands of disabled people throughout the world is a miracle in itself.

ISBN: 978-1-85792-833-4

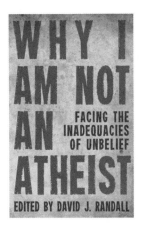

Eleven Christians — including a biologist, a psychiatrist, a journalist, and a debater — travelled on eleven diverse paths to faith in Jesus Christ. This book is the compilation of their answers and experiences written in response to Bertrand Russell's *Why I Am Not A Christian*.

ISBN: 978-1-78191-270-6

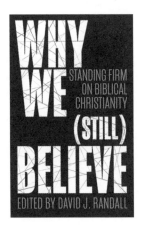

The West has become permeated with a culture that doesn't 'do' God. Many people assert that we have progressed, while Christians are still clinging to out-dated ideas. In *Why We (Still) Believe*, fourteen contributors focus on several specific contemporary attacks on Christianity, showing why they 'continue in the faith' (Col.1:23).

ISBN: 978-1-5271-0088-6

CHRISTIAN FOCUS PUBLICATIONS

Christian Christian CF4K Mentor
Focus Heritage

Christian Focus Publications publishes books for adults and children under its four main imprints: Christian Focus, CF4K, Mentor and Christian Heritage. Our books reflect our conviction that God's Word is reliable and Jesus is the way to know him, and live for ever with him.

Our children's publication list includes a Sunday school curriculum that covers pre-school to early teens, and puzzle and activity books. We also publish personal and family devotional titles, biographies and inspirational stories that children will love.

If you are looking for quality Bible teaching for children then we have an excellent range of Bible stories and age-specific theological books.

From pre-school board books to teenage apologetics, we have it covered!

Find us at our web page:
www.christianfocus.com

CF4•K
*Because you're never
too young to know Jesus*